I0062927

Live A Healthy, Happy, Long Life and Prosper Without Stress

THE LIFE TRANSFORMATION PARADIGM:

SEVEN LIFESTYLE SHIFTS TO LIVE THE LIFE YOU ARE DESIGNED TO LIVE

Live A Healthy, Happy, Long Life and Prosper Without Stress

THE LIFE TRANSFORMATION PARADIGM:

SEVEN LIFESTYLE SHIFTS TO LIVE THE LIFE
YOU ARE DESIGNED TO LIVE

Jose M. Baltazar, PhD

Copyright © 2021 by Jose M. Baltazar, PhD

All rights reserved. No part of this book may be used or reproduced in any manner whatsoever without prior written consent of the authors, except as provided by the United States of America copyright law.

Published by Best Seller Publishing®, Pasadena, CA
Best Seller Publishing® is a registered trademark.
Printed in the United States of America.
ISBN: 978-1-949535-89-1

This publication is designed to provide accurate and authoritative information with regard to the subject matter covered. It is sold with the understanding that the publisher is not engaged in rendering legal, accounting, or other professional advice. If legal advice or other expert assistance is required, the services of a competent professional should be sought. The opinions expressed by the authors in this book are not endorsed by Best Seller Publishing® and are the sole responsibility of the author rendering the opinion.

For more information, please write:
Best Seller Publishing®
253 N. San Gabriel Blvd, Unit B
Pasadena, CA 91107
or call 1 (626) 765 9750
Visit us online at: www.BestSellerPublishing.org

TABLE OF CONTENTS

A Special Invitation to You.
A Better Way to Live.

"After all is said and done, in life, health, and longevity are of most importance."

— Dr. Jose M. Baltazar

I am writing this foreword as a special invitation to you to keep reading this book.

We are designed to live a life of happiness and peace. Happiness and peace allow us to live healthy, long, and prosperously.

There are different ways to pursue happiness and peace, but most ways take you to the wrong destination. The most prevalent models or paradigms emphasize the "work hard" ethic, with the focus on accumulation of money, leading you to believe that by working hard to accumulate money, you eventually will be able to live the peaceful and happy life you seek and want.

The emphasis on the accumulation or earning of money to achieve peace and happiness has created a society and a world in which everyone is running around overly busy and stressed and overloaded with responsibility. At the end, most cannot find peace and happiness because they are in too much debt or are chronically ill at a younger age. Most do not come out winners in the accumulation game. We are a sickened society from the results of so much stress from pursuing peace and happiness by following the wrong paradigm of living.

There is a different way, a different model. I call this model The Life Transformation Paradigm.

The Life Transformation Paradigm helps you find peace and happiness first, so that the other things everyone wants more of can be obtained with much less effort and stress. The Life Transformation Paradigm turns conventional wisdom on its head. First you find and enjoy peace and happiness, and then you can live the life you are designed to live. You are designed to live happily and at peace — a healthy, long, and prosperous life.

This book is about my model and how to work with it so you can start living the life you are designed to live. I have lived by this model since my early thirties. I am almost seventy and, take it from me and the thousands of other people I have taught and coached to follow my model — it works.

The Life Transformation Paradigm works because it is a system of living and requires shifts in how you are living life for each of seven components. You may have integrated some of its components into living your life already, but as I have found out through my years of living by this model, teaching it, and coaching people through it, most individuals are lacking more than one required shift. Once you make all the shifts necessary, you will be living your life the way you are designed to live it: at peace while living a happy, healthy, long, and prosperous life.

In addition, the second part of this foreword is written by a longtime friend of mine whom I admire for her ability to create and sustain a lifestyle exactly like the one this book guides you to live. She is truly living a happy, healthy, long, and prosperous life.

I am writing this book as the second wave of the coronavirus pandemic has just started.

When I started writing it, I never thought it would be published in a situation when everyone's lives are being affected so negatively. I pray and hope your life is not one of the lives that has been affected so badly.

During this time, cases of mental illness, anxiety, depression, sadness, despair, and suicide have increased significantly. The number of divorces and amount of strain in family relationships have also drastically increased. And the recovery from the pandemic is also projected to be long and arduous, especially for those of us who are not among the "rich and famous."

The message of this book is timeless, and currently it is more relevant than ever before.

Everyone is going through the pandemic and so eagerly waiting for a vaccine, hoping that will mark the end of it. However, when the pandemic is over, all of us will need to work ourselves out of the leftover effects and heal ourselves from them. The pandemic has added additional stress to our lives in more than one area, whether it be financial, employment, relationships, peace and health of mind, body, and spirit, and so on.

This book is a guide for living a happy, healthy, long, prosperous, and stress-free life.

These are the desires of most people, whether there is a pandemic or not. The pandemic has highlighted these basic needs for just about everyone. We need to heed the message it has brought us. In this book, I will share with you a model of how to live the life you want to live and, most importantly, with minimum stress and without the health ravages a stressful lifestyle brings.

Before the pandemic, we were living highly stressful lives. We got so used to being in a hurry all the time, taking the kids around to many places. In the hurry to get them there on time, we got used to eating unhealthy fast food frequently, and we did all this after working eight- to twelve-hour shifts. We also got so busy taking care of social issues, political campaigns, causes to protect our environment, and a whole list of other things. Please do not get me wrong. All these things are good; however, in the process, we put ourselves under so much pressure and stress that stress itself became a pandemic. Stress is, and has been for decades, the major factor for all our physical, and mental illnesses. Unless we make healthy shifts in our lifestyles, this will continue to be true, even after the pandemic.

The pandemic stopped us in our tracks and forced us to live life at a slower pace.

This happened globally and at a high cost to societies and their economies. By publication time we had lived through it almost a year, and it was projected it would continue at least halfway through 2021, if not longer. There are many lessons to learn from this period of adversity, but one of the principal lessons to learn is what this book teaches: how living a happy, healthy, long, and prosperous life without so much stress and its damaging effects is possible. After all, this is the life we were meant and designed to live. My friend Bertha is a living model of this lifestyle. This is the reason I asked her to write the second part of this foreword. Bertha is a retired public school counselor and teaches at El Paso Community College. I met her more than 20 years ago. Since then, she has participated in most of my workshops and programs, and she gives much credit to my teachings for the improvements she has brought to her live.

BERTHA, AN EXAMPLE OF LIVING BY THE
LIFE TRANSFORMATION PARADIGM

It is not uncommon these days to come across people who suffer from some sort of ailment that afflicts them. Consider how many of us resort to spending a fortune on over-the-counter or prescribed drugs and procedures that may promise quick relief and appear to be an answer to our prayers. At times, we become disappointed to find that the solution is temporary or may come with costly side effects on our health.

Live a Happy, Healthy, Long Life and Prosper Without Stress by Dr. Jose Baltazar offers an opportunity to strike a balance between your mind, body, and spirit as you gain more power and control over your health and entire life. You will be provided with the tools to learn to relax, meditate, and pay attention to what your body is telling you. The longer you relax, the deeper the healing process in your mind and body will be. Be open-minded and become curious about Dr. Baltazar's "Life Transformation Paradigm — Seven Lifestyle Shifts to Live the Life You Are Designed to Live." Answer his invitation to live a healthy, stress-free life by practicing the strategies he provides in this book. Consider how you will feel once you obtain a stronger immune system and great health without the need for medication!

Dr. Baltazar's model will provide a clear image of the life you are designed to live. He will help you become aware of the need for self-care so you can live a healthy and productive life. His techniques will help you begin your day by reducing stressful situations and consciously choosing to live a life of peace. With self-care practice, you will rewire your brain and train your mind to heal and maintain a healthy internal dialogue that will allow you to live by choice and not by chance.

I can attest to Dr. Baltazar's "Life Transformation Paradigm — Seven Lifestyle Shifts to Live the Life You Are Designed to Live" and can happily say that meditation, imagery, affirmations, relaxation, the power of breath, and positive attitude have helped me change my life for the better. His method has not only raised my consciousness but has also healed my strained relationships and attracted a loving, mature relationship to my life. I can now think outside the box and have gained the courage to challenge and modify my beliefs, my agreements, and even my own identity. In the process, I am creating a new reality. I am no longer stuck in old patterns and now pay attention to my thinking patterns in a manner that is free from regret, shame, or guilt. I am able to dream new dreams. As I weigh the possibilities of living a life without restrictions, I find that Dr. Jose Baltazar's optimism and positive outlook have motivated me to watch my life unfold effortlessly, in a most magnificent way.

— Bertha Orona, educator

ADVERSITY

There are two ways you can look at adversity.
One is to fret, cry, and get depressed and
become pessimistic and frustrated due to it.
The other is to learn, adjust, be hopeful,
grow, and improve because of it.

Every adversity offers the opportunity to
fail, give up, and be unhappy, or to keep being hopeful
and under pressure come out victorious.
Adversity is the test that we must pass or fail
to consider ourselves a success or a failure in life.

Accept adversity optimistically when it comes to you,
for if you face it head-on, patiently, with faith,
and without complaint,
you will become a better person,
and then, and only then,
you will know the true meaning of success.

— Dr. Jose M. Baltazar

You Were Designed to Thrive, Not Just to Survive

- Are you facing a difficult time in your life?

- Do you wish that life were not so stressful?

- Do you have any goals that seem to elude you?

- Do you feel like you are running around too much and making little or no progress?

- Do you feel frustrated about the way your life is?

- Do you wish your relationships were better?

- Do you frequently feel tired and/or exhausted?

- Does your health need improvement?

- Do you wish you were making more money or had a better job or career?

- Do you have bigger dreams or desires that seem unreachable or too far away?

- Do you consider yourself successful but wish to achieve greater successes?

If you answered "yes" to any of these questions, this book is for you. You will benefit greatly by changing your lifestyle to live it within my Life Transformation Paradigm model. Even if you answered "no" to all the questions, I am certain you will learn information that will help you make your life even better. In this book, I will share with you how my model helps you live the life you desire and that you are intended to live. I have been using this system of personal growth and self-improvement for over thirty years. Living according to this model has helped me pursue all my dreams and achieve every single one, all without the damaging effects of stress, and keep up excellent relationships, remain in excellent health, keep my levels of energy much higher than the average sixty-nine-year-old, and enjoy financial freedom since my early thirties. I still have dreams and goals, which I am certain I will achieve.

I have taught my model to diverse populations. I have used it with people of all ages, creeds, races, professions, and socioeconomic statuses, and it has proven effective for them. I have taught my system to teachers and parents so they can use it on themselves and their children and students, and they also report effective results. I have conducted four studies, two with a control group in them. These studies demonstrate my system to be effective. But what excites me the most is the hundreds of testimonials I have collected through the years. I will share my journey with you in this book by sharing some of the stories that have inspired me to share my model with you. Through all the experiences like the ones I will share with you here, I have developed a personal mission to help people accomplish their goals and desires faster and more easily, with minimum stress and excellent health and wellness benefits. I have accomplished my mission through my Life Transformation Paradigm.

LEARNING THROUGH NEAR-DEATH — MY STORY

My journey of transformation started in 1978. I was twenty-four years old and was doing well in the information technology industry. In four short years, I had risen to making a salary I never thought I would be making in such a short time. I had moved up quickly to enjoy the lifestyle of the high middle class and had become a role model for other Hispanics in the city in which I lived.

Economic success had not come easily. In the process of growing up with high aspirations of improving my own life, I had developed a high achiever's mentality, which to me meant working hard, long hours and living my life in hyperactive mode. I was married, with two children, but I was not paying much attention to my marriage nor my two children. One day in 1980, my wife approached me and told me that unless I changed and realigned my priorities, she was not going to stay in the marriage much longer.

Her body language told me she was serious, so I decided to change my hyperactive approach to my career. I started attending church more, taking Bible study classes, and becoming more involved in building up my relationship with my wife and children. I stopped working so much, but now was so busy being involved in church activities and volunteer work that I ended up again living my own hyperactive lifestyle. The only difference was that my wife was involved and so were my children. For a while, it seemed like things were looking up.

In 1983 I caught a strong flu and cold that knocked me down and would not go away for four days, despite my taking flu and cold over-the-counter medicines. Suddenly, on the evening of the fourth day, my entire body was in intolerable pain, and I could not move my head in any direction because if I did, it would hurt like it was going to explode. The pain got totally unbearable, and I asked my wife to take me to the hospital. At the hospital, the nurse looked at me and called the doctor, and they took me in right away. I just remember the doctor saying it looked like I had meningitis. After that, I do not remember anything else until I woke up one week later in quarantine. Later, the doctor came in and spoke to me. He said I was lucky and that if I had come in five minutes later, he would not have been able to do anything for me. It was meningitis.

WE BELIEVE GREATER SUCCESS IS HARD, SO WE SETTLE AND STRUGGLE

Often, we want to change something within us or in our external life. We know life could be much better, but we get used to functioning within our comfort zone. We like to feel safe and even though we know life would be better if we changed it, our false beliefs, insecurities, and the possibility of failure holds us back. Until suddenly some extremely bad experience forces us to change, or someone who cares about and believes in us comes along and provides us with the support and encouragement to move forward and take the risk.

I have taught and coached many individuals who were struggling in their lives. They were trying to make higher incomes, get higher grades, change careers, enter highly selective universities, improve their marriages, pass exams to be able to practice their professions, and make many other changes to improve their lives. I found in most cases that they were struggling because they did not know or were not willing to make necessary changes in themselves to be able to move forward and excel.

My father, although he did not complete school beyond the sixth grade, was a successful small business entrepreneur. He taught me a simple and effective model of success. He taught me that to achieve any higher goal successfully, three things were needed: skills, resources, and attitude.

He would explain that if you want to have a successful business, you need to learn the **skills** for the kind of business you want to have as well as the skills needed to run a business successfully. You also need to have **resources** like money, but most importantly, you need to get to know people who own successful businesses. They are your best resource because they will teach you, guide you, and even lend you money to get started. You also need to learn how they think (**attitude**). How they face tough times, how they feel about the business they have, and why they are willing to work long hours and work so hard. The belief he was transferring to me was that success was hard work.

That formula has helped me tremendously in my own life . . . but there was something still lacking. The one answer I could not get when I kept asking, "Why does being successful have to be so stressful and hard?" Everyone I asked would tell me it was because that is what being more successful requires — hard work and lots of stress. Most people have this belief. Success is hard work. And they live their lives demonstrating this belief in their daily routine.

Even today I see it all over the place. People are busier than ever, and because it is more expensive than ever to live, most people are running around taking care of daily life and end their day tired and exhausted. Technology is supposed to make things easier, and it seems to be having the opposite effect. To top it off, people are getting sicker and sicker. Even kids nowadays are developing chronic diseases at a much younger age and at a faster rate than ever before. What is happening?!

YOU CAN BE BUSY, BUT YOU DO NOT HAVE TO SUFFER THE RAVAGES OF STRESS

Back to my near-death experience. After a week of being unconscious and having been five minutes away from death, I woke up in quarantine. The doctor was at my bedside and asked me a few questions about my lifestyle. He said that I had contracted a meningitis infection and went on to explain how it had developed from the cold I got.

My immune system had not been able to fight it because it was weak from my high stress levels. He also said that only time could tell if there were going to be any long-term effects on my brain functioning or any physical symptoms expressed by my nervous system. Then he advised me to be thankful I was alive and recommended I change my lifestyle and to learn to relax. "Learn to take it easier," he said. "Next time you may not be so lucky."

I finally learned my lesson. I had already gotten my master's degree in human and organization developmental psychology and decided to work at improving my coaching and teaching skills. I also decided to improve myself and my personal lifestyle, and to immerse myself in the self-help field with the intention to change myself to be able to live life with less stress.

Thinking that my hyperactive and stressed life was due to my being in a career that by nature was stressful, I started planning a change of occupation. I liked helping people improve their lives by getting a college education. I was already teaching classes in data processing. I was also learning and incorporating many of the helpful personal development strategies I was learning into my own life, so I decided to get into the counseling and teaching profession.

In 1987, I decided to quit the information technology field and left the high-tech management job I had in the college I was working for in California. Changing careers from high-tech management to counseling and teaching meant taking a big cut in pay. To be able to afford the change, I had to move my family to an area in the United States where the cost of living was lower. After thinking, talking, and planning, my wife and I agreed that we would move to the city of El Paso, Texas, a border town community.

Changing careers and moving to El Paso would prove to be of great significance in my life. Being a teacher and a counselor would lead me to develop a lifestyle that was by choice busy and stressful and, to top it off, not as highly paid as high-tech management. Busy and stressful, yes, for most people — however, I found my new career to be fulfilling and enjoyable. I discovered I loved helping people improve their lives through education and personal development. I loved the fact that by helping others improve themselves, I was improving myself as well.

As part of my own learning and development, I discovered ways to be relaxed and highly productive under heavy pressure and stress. The ability to relax under stress made me one of the most creative and productive members of the faculty at El Paso Community College. I spent thirty years creating and developing programs and curriculum and providing counseling and coaching that helped thousands of students overcome difficult obstacles and be successful in their educational endeavors.

Through the years, I learned and developed a system of success that allowed me and others with whom I shared it to perform difficult tasks and achieve higher dreams and goals while being able to remain relaxed, focused, and healthy. This system allows people to exhibit high levels of performance while being unstressed and remaining healthy.

This is the system I will share with you in this book. At the same time, I will teach you most of the techniques I teach students, professionals, and clients to be able to accomplish their dreams, desires, and goals in all areas of their lives while, most importantly, remaining healthy and avoiding the detrimental effects stress causes. I call this lifestyle model The Life Transformation Paradigm. It will transform your life. Life can keep getting more stressful, and it will, but you will prevent stress from affecting you, and you will be healthy enough to enjoy life and your accomplishments. *You will live a happy, healthy, long life and prosper without stress.*

CHAPTER 1

The Life Transformation Paradigm: The Seven Lifestyle Shifts That Will Transform Your Life

"We see the world, not as it is, but as we are — or, as we are conditioned to see it."

— Stephen R. Covey,
The 7 Habits of Highly Effective People

LISTEN TO EXPERTS, BUT DO NOT BELIEVE EVERYTHING THEY SUGGEST

Mary was a failing college student in her twenties who was sent to me with a diagnosis of learning disabilities longer than a weekly grocery list. She started crying as soon as she came into my office. She had just been told by a psychologist to forget about becoming a teacher and to settle for a shorter and easier career choice. I enrolled Mary in my student success course and worked with her a few times individually. In less than a year, she raised her grade point average to 3.5 and became the president of the Honors Society.

The last time I saw Mary, she was already working as an elementary school teacher, and later went on to work as a trainer at an aerospace company. Below is a portion of a letter of appreciation she wrote to me:

I learned a lot about accelerated learning and how to succeed in life from Mr. Baltazar's lifestyle model. I started practicing the techniques he taught me. I used to be a "C" or "D" student and now my grades have improved to "A" and "B." Mr. Baltazar taught me very helpful techniques that started working for me right away. I decided to enroll in his Accelerated Learning Study Skills class. I have learned many more techniques that help me emotionally, physically, as well as academically. I am very thankful to Mr. Baltazar for all the help he has given me.

CREATING HABITS TO REALIZE YOUR DESIRES

You know how people make resolutions for the new year? You have probably made some resolutions for the new year yourself. I used to do this, but stopped many years ago. Reality tells us that most people will not follow through with them. At best, they will get started and soon thereafter go back to the usual behaviors. This also happens to most people who set goals. Estimates go as far as showing that close to 80 percent of people who set goals will not achieve them. Most do not realize that to achieve higher goals and desires, what are needed are better habits of behavior. The keyword is "habits."

Your life at present is the way it is because of your habits. Habits are behaviors driven by beliefs that have been developed through frequent exposure and repetition. Every human being has needs, wants, and desires of different types. They can be material, physical, emotional, or spiritual. Wanting, needing, and desiring more is natural and innate to humans. Needs, desires, and wants are the essence of existence and the manifestation that we are born to thrive and not just survive. We are meant to continue learning, growing, and contributing, and doing it better than before. To thrive, we must continue to develop new, and improve our current, attitudes, behaviors, and skills. We must continue to develop new habits and improve our current ones. Habits make up the totality of our lives.

LIFE IMPROVES WHEN YOU IMPROVE
YOUR BELIEFS AND YOUR HABITS

Pat was working at a community college as a paraprofessional in the social work and counseling fields. She was in her late thirties and had always dreamed of becoming a counselor for the same institution. When I met Pat, she shared her dream with me but would always end stating that it was too late, she was not smart enough, she hated doing homework, it would take forever to get a counselor position even if she got her master's degree, etc. These beliefs led Pat to develop habits of thinking and behavior that stopped her from realizing her higher dreams. Although she had attempted to before — more than one time, so far — she had not been able to achieve them.

I invited Pat to work with me, and after five sessions she made the decision to enroll in a counseling master's program, completed it with honors, got the counseling position she wanted, and has received numerous awards as a community volunteer and special recognitions as a faculty member. She became an administrator and has run one of the counseling centers at the same institution for over five years. Pat also teaches Student Success courses and has become one of my best friends and a promoter of my approach for coaching people to greater success, achievement, and fulfillment.

THE LIFE TRANSFORMATION PARADIGM
— A MINDSET AND LIFESTYLE

For over forty-four years, I worked mostly with college and university students, and professionals wanting to overcome obstacles that seemed to hold them back from moving on to the next step in achieving worthwhile goals and dreams. For the past ten years, I have also worked with people suffering from mental illness, weight issues, trauma, financial problems, career/job concerns, financial concerns, relationship problems, spiritual issues, and physical illness. I have used my model to help them overcome their situations and move forward in their lives successfully.

Why is my model effective? I believe it is because of its holistic, systemic, and non-cognitive approach to personal change and improvement. Most life coaches, in my experience, preach the holistic approach, but in implementation their coaching interventions address only the issue at hand, almost the same as the medical system. In addition, most techniques (I prefer calling them interventions) they teach are cognitive in nature. Cognitive interventions take a long time and lots of work to bring about small changes. I use mostly non-cognitive interventions which target change at a deep level in the subconscious. Subconscious (non-cognitive) interventions are much more powerful, and effect change without much effort and in much less time. Improvements in beliefs and habits of behavior happen much quicker when done at the subconscious level as well. This is how Maria and Pat were able to make changes in their behavior to be able to achieve their higher desires after struggling for years.

THE SCIENCE BEHIND THE MODEL — NEUROSCIENCE AND NEUROPLASTICITY

For over thirty years, I have experienced the most joy and satisfaction in my career because of a discovery I made back in 1990. After delving into traditional training and teaching pedagogy and approaches and noticing that regardless of how much money in financial aid the government provided, my research showed that the graduation rates in colleges and universities, except elite ones, oscillated between 20 percent and 25 percent, while the high school drop-out rate was a staggering 50 percent. I decided to look into alternative and non-traditional approaches to teaching and learning.

In 1990, I ran into a methodology of learning called accelerated learning while attempting to help a bright student (A/B grade average). She had been kicked out of the nursing program at my institution because she was not able to sustain the A/B average required by the health programs. In addition, her liver had actually ripped open due to the stress and demands of the program.

In my research, I saw a reference to a book titled *Super-Learning* (Ostrander and Schroeder 1982). This book changed my life and the lives of hundreds of my students. It started my journey of learning about the most miraculous organ in our bodies: the brain. I read it from beginning to end over a weekend and extracted some of the techniques the authors shared. I taught the student how to relax under stress, how to use relaxing music while studying, and a powerful technique you will learn in this book called autogenics. I asked her to practice them for two weeks. She came back after two weeks looking happy, healthy, and excited. She had her little girl with her, who was listening to music on her Walkman cassette player (. . . remember those?). She gave me a hug and thanked me. She had been accepted back into the nursing program. She had taken the reentrance test, had passed it, and was looking forward to getting back into her nursing studies.

Then she asked me a question: what do you think my daughter is listening to? "What?" I asked. She told me her daughter had been listening to the music I had asked her to use as part of the technique I had taught her. She stated that her daughter was diagnosed with attention deficit disorder (ADD) and that her daughter's teacher had communicated to her that lately she had been so focused on her classes and was getting good grades. Since then, I have seen other "miracles" in performance improvements in other people I have coached that are too many to describe. I knew I had run into something special and powerful to help people become better learners and achievers.

By the way, my nursing student came back at the end of the semester to show me her report card. She had gotten As in all but one of her courses, where she got a B.

I started researching the field of accelerated learning in more depth. This method of teaching and learning taught me many of the techniques I will share with you in this book. I bought many books and training manuals and started attending conferences and certification trainings in the field. I have had many more significant experiences in helping people that have shaped me and have contributed to the development of my model, The Life Transformation Paradigm.

What I had learned so far through accelerated learning was that in addition to being able to achieve goals faster and easier, people also obtained mental and physical health benefits. My students and clients would frequently share with me that besides being able to overcome obstacles in their progress toward their goals, they were experiencing health benefits such as relief from low back pain and headaches, sleeping much better, regulating high blood pressure, and more.

In my most recent experience, I have become immersed in the field of mind-body medicine and earned my PhD in this science. This experience taught me why my clients and students were experiencing health benefits in addition to getting their goals realized. Getting my PhD in mind-body medicine has expanded my understanding of the brain and cemented my belief in the power of the human being to live a happier, more prosperous, and more high-achieving life while remaining healthy and not experiencing so much unhealthy stress.

THE LIFE TRANSFORMATION PARADIGM: THE WAY TO RELAXED AND ACCELERATED SUCCESS

Accelerated learning is a system of learning in which the emphasis is on knowledge of how the brain learns best. Based on that knowledge, we learn and develop learning interventions or techniques that help individuals learn better and faster. My Life Transformation Paradigm is based on accelerated learning and mind-body medicine principles. By combining these two philosophies into a style of living, one is capable of functioning effectively and efficiently in all areas of life. You can live stress-free while being highly productive, healthy, and successful at living your own life.

My transformation model has at its core the science of relaxation and meditation. I practiced relaxation and meditation since early in my thirties, but I was not aware of the science behind it. I became familiar with the law of attraction before I became familiar with the science that makes it work. You have probably seen the movie and have heard all of the motivating phrases that imply the power behind the law of attraction. Here are some phrases we have been hearing for a long time:

- "Whatever your mind can conceive and believe, you can achieve." — Napoleon Hill

- "The ability of the individual to think is his ability to act on the Universal and bring it into manifestation." — Charles F. Haanel

- "Success is determined not so much by the size of one's brain as it is by the size of one's thinking." — David J. Schwartz

- "Whether you think you can or you think you can't, you are right." — Henry Ford

- "Therefore I tell you, all that you ask for in prayer, believe that you will receive it and it shall be yours." — Mark 11:24 (NABRE; St. Joseph MEDIUM SIZE Edition)

The *Law of Attraction* movie showed us that to get what we want, we need to visualize it vividly in our mind and feel the feelings we would experience as if we already had that which we want.

All these philosophical ways of thinking are right and true. A critical factor, however, has been left out when the philosophies are taught to other people. It is interesting to me that even though I had been working at improving my own life for many years, until I ran into accelerated learning, no one had placed emphases on the science of relaxation and meditation as a way of speeding up change. The science behind mind-body medicine explains why the law of attraction works. There is an amazing power we possess that has been naturally given to each of us. This power is our brain and our mind. Unfortunately, few people know how to use this power to manage their life. Even most people who are considered intelligent lack knowledge of how to systemically and holistically use their mind to improve their lives. Some get rich and end up sick and unhappy. Some are outstanding in their fields and suffer loneliness and depression. In this book, I will share with you how you can live your life feeling happy, being healthy, and achieving all your desires.

Empowered and inspired by the results of my own studies and hundreds of documented testimonials, I have developed my holistic and integrated Life Transformation Paradigm. The following is a diagram of the model and a brief description of each component. The sequencing of the components is not critical. The only component to learn and practice before the others is the central and foundational principle of relaxation and meditation. The other components work in tandem with each other. In practicing them, you will always rely on relaxation and meditation to increase their effectiveness. You will naturally use all of them as you face your daily life's circumstances and challenges.

THE LIFE TRANSFORMATION PARADIGM:
AN OVERVIEW

COPYRIGHT © BY JOSE M. BALTAZAR, PHD

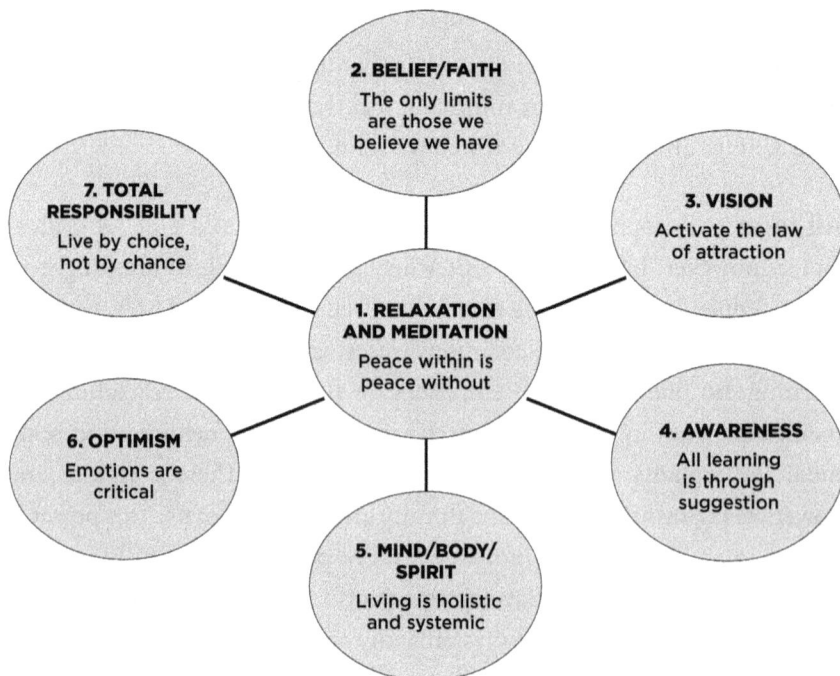

2. BELIEF/FAITH
The only limits are those we believe we have

7. TOTAL RESPONSIBILITY
Live by choice, not by chance

3. VISION
Activate the law of attraction

1. RELAXATION AND MEDITATION
Peace within is peace without

6. OPTIMISM
Emotions are critical

4. AWARENESS
All learning is through suggestion

5. MIND/BODY/ SPIRIT
Living is holistic and systemic

Lifestyle Shift #1: Relaxation and Meditation (The Core)

The brain is the master organ that drives our behavior. To reprogram it for more productive behaviors, it must be at the highest level of receptiveness possible. The more receptive the brain is, the easier it is for it to develop new or improve positive behaviors. Because all the other components of my model require changes in behavior, you can see why this component is so critical. Through a menu of mind-body techniques such as imagery, autogenics, self-hypnosis, neurolinguistics, the relaxation response, mindfulness, transcendental meditation, brain wave management, sub-conscious learning, and others, personal change occurs much faster and easier. This menu of mind-body medicine approaches makes my model powerful and effective.

Lifestyle Shift #2: Faith/Belief

Changing and improving beliefs is one of the first lessons of most motivators and teachers of success. Everyone agrees with the principle of believing in oneself and in the dream or goal we desire. No matter how successful they are, they can benefit from strengthening their belief in themselves and in their potential to achieve what they desire. Most recommendations and approaches to improve beliefs depend on cognitive processes. Through relaxation and meditation exercises that target improvement in self-belief, change becomes non-cognitive and penetrates deeper into the subconscious to effectuate change faster and with minimum effort.

Lifestyle Shift #3: Vision

We have visions of what we want and wish to obtain. Some visions are unclear; others are pursued with doubt, even though people want them. Others have clear visions of what they want and yet are unable to obtain it. What is the difference between those who realize their dreams and desires and those who struggle to or never obtain them? Success requires consistency of positive emotion, such as excitement and optimism, toward their vision. Relaxation and meditation are vehicles to sustain relaxed and calm excitement and action towards realizing dreams and desires.

Lifestyle Shift #4: Awareness

One of the essential factors of success is attention and concentration of effort. This is also referred to as focus. This skill and this behavior are naturally developed by the practice of relaxation and meditation techniques. In addition, there are specific strategies to increase focus and awareness that, when integrated with relaxation and meditation, accelerate the development of greater awareness, attention, and focus. I teach these strategies as part of adapting my Life Transformation Paradigm lifestyle.

Lifestyle Shift #5: Mind-Body-Spirit

The mind, the body, and the spirit of a human being are one. This is a holistic principle of systems. If any one of the components is not properly taken care of, the health and performance of the system suffers and slows down significantly or deteriorates at a faster rate. Meditation and relaxation processes integrate the mind, body, and spirit of the person and develop motivation to take good care of each component to maintain high levels of energy and productivity.

Lifestyle Shift #6: Optimism

Optimism is an attitude and a skill. Optimistic people tend to be more successful than the average person. It helps anyone to learn to be more optimistic by using mental models and procedures that transform a person into a more optimistic one. Dr. Martin E.P. Seligman of the University of Pennsylvania teaches ways to be more optimistic in his book, *Learned Optimism: How to Change Your Mind and Your Life.* Learning these approaches, supported by relaxation and meditation, makes the learning and changing process much easier and faster.

Lifestyle Shift #7: Total Responsibility

Taking total responsibility for the choices we make, without excuses and without blaming anyone when things do not go our way, is a major change for most people. When things do not turn out the way we expected, the tendency is to blame someone else or look for causes outside of our control. This way, we feel excused for things not going our way. By living life with total responsibility, this focuses energy upon the individual and empowers him/her with the flexibility to make new and better choices. Once again, relaxation and meditation in my model facilitate the needed change in thinking and behavior to live life with total responsibility.

There you have it. These are the seven shifts to help you live a more fulfilling and abundant life. I have been teaching and coaching clients individually and in group sessions and class settings, helping them to run their lives according to this model for over twenty-five years. I am encouraged by the positive feedback I continue to receive, and by the results of studies I have recently conducted.

The one component that you will resort to throughout your day and in every circumstance will be relaxation and meditation. I know — it sounds like you will have to spend your day sitting down meditating and relaxing. That is not so; you will learn to be relaxed and rested while busy under the pressures of your day. You will also be able to sleep deeply and peacefully when you decide it is time to go to bed.

Keep reading. You are in for a pleasant and joyful ride for the rest of your life.

CHAPTER 2

Lifestyle Shift #1: Relaxation and Meditation— Peace Within Is Peace Without

Part 1: Stress Is the Greatest Obstacle to Living the Life You Are Designed to Live

"Stress is nothing more than a socially acceptable form of mental illness."

— Richard Carlson

Klara, a young intern at one of our local hospitals, was referred to me because after trying two times, she had not been able to pass her medical exam and she was running out of options as to what else to try before her next scheduled exam. Could I help her? A friend of hers had given her my name because I had been able to help other professionals pass their license examinations. I asked her to give me a rundown of how she had prepared for the test before. She related the typical process to me: long nights of studying, frequent reviews, lots of repetition, and above all lots of stress. To add to her frustration, she had missed the passing scores by only three or five points.

Klara had been successful at gaining acceptance to medical school. She had graduated with excellent grades and had been able to meet all other demands in her life, and now her professional life was in jeopardy. Imagine, after all that work, not being able to realize her ultimate dream and desire — practice as a physician.

I have seen and worked with many clients and students going through the same situation. They are attempting to reach a higher level of performance with the same skills and behaviors that have gotten them to where they are at present. They suddenly come to a point where they cannot get beyond by trying harder at doing what they have done before. Many succeed, but at a high cost to their health and emotional stability. Unfortunately, many quit and settle for something less than what they desire in their heart. They go on living, resigned to their failure, never feeling fulfilled and considering themselves not equipped to realize their more ambitious dreams.

People struggle to make permanent changes in their lives and to achieve their higher desires and dreams because they depend on cognitive processes and the force of the will. That will only take you so far. What you need is to make shifts in your lifestyle that will make a big difference in the outcomes you desire. These shifts do not have to be major changes, just small shifts that make a major difference.

RELAXATION AND MEDITATION: THE CORE LIFESTYLE SHIFT

In my Life Transformation Paradigm model, I propose that relaxation and meditation need to be at the core of our existence and thus are habits that all humans should develop. Relaxation and meditation are the vehicles by which higher dreams and desires can be accomplished, good habits can be improved upon, and new ones can be developed without struggle. Relaxation and meditation will help you live a busy and demanding life while remaining healthy and free from the stress of a busy lifestyle. Relaxation and meditation will help you live a balanced and healthy emotional life, make your relationships healthier and more successful and your decisions and choices more accurate. Relaxation and meditation are the core contributors to living a happy, healthy, longer, peaceful, prosperous, and fulfilled life.

YOU DO NOT HAVE TO BECOME BUDDHA, OR LIVE IN RETREAT IN A CONVENT OR MONASTERY

There are two major reasons for learning to relax and meditate:

a.   To reduce stress and to allow you to feel rested and at peace, and to think more logically and make time for your mind, body, and spirit to regenerate and achieve balance.

b   To place your brain (mind) in a more receptive state for accepting information and commands in the subconscious that transform your state of mind into more productive emotions and behaviors. When you remain calm, cool, and collected in stressful circumstances, you remain healthier, full of energy, and emotionally in control. You become more productive and much more prosperous in every area of your life.

Relaxation and meditation are frequently associated with Eastern religious practices. Many people seeking peace within themselves tend to retreat to special places in Eastern countries to learn and integrate their religious traditions and practices. Some even convert to and adapt these practices as their religion. Many people are hesitant and shy away from the practice because they think whoever teaches them will attempt to influence them to change whatever spiritual practices they already have.

Relaxation and meditation have become sciences themselves. Since the 1960s, these practices have been studied at many of the most highly recognized universities throughout the world (*Biofeedback: A Practitioner's Guide* by Mark S. Schwartz and Frank Andrasik). One of the concepts in brain science that has been popularized by research using biofeedback devices is brain wave technology. Research has demonstrated that our brains function at different frequencies depending on the activities and emotional states we experience while performing such activities (*Brain States Mastery* by Brian M. Morrissey). With this information, we can learn to manage and induce these brain waves in our brains and thus help our minds to work more efficiently.

BRAIN WAVE DESCRIPTIONS AND ACTIVITIES THAT GENERATE THEM

The brain works in different frequencies, and it accepts information in all of them. Depending in what frequency the brain is when it receives information determines how quickly and strongly the information is recorded. This is important knowledge when you are trying to learn new information and behaviors. The deeper you relax the better and faster the information or commands will register in your subconscious, increasing the speed and the permanency of the behavior changes you are trying to make.

Below I describe the different brain frequencies. The slower the frequency, the deeper and more relaxed you are and the faster and more permanently information goes into your subconscious. This is one of the reasons I use relaxation and meditation as the foundation for the Life Transformation Paradigm. In the meditative state, your brain functions at the alpha/theta level thus helping your mind accept information easier, faster, and deeper. This is one of the reasons why meditation is so helpful to reduce stress, helps the mind and body heal, and re-conditions the brain for better and healthier behaviors.

FIVE BASIC BRAINWAVE FREQUENCIES

The brain functions in five basic frequencies. Each frequency runs at a specific range measured in hertz (cycles per second). Everyone experiences these frequencies, but most people are unaware when this is happening. They notice how their mental and physical states change because they experience these changes through their bodies and their emotions, but they are unaware of what is happening within their brains.

There are five brain frequencies neuroscientists have been able to identify. Basic familiarity with these frequencies empowers us to exercise more control over our brain and our minds. The ability to control these frequencies at will is called brain-wave management.

The slower the frequency, the easier it becomes for the brain to take in, process, comprehend, and store information. Knowing how to place our brains in these frequencies on demand, empowers us to change ourselves much quicker and faster. Following is a brief explanation of each brain frequency. If you are interested in learning more details, please visit the following link: binauralbeatsonline.com

The five brain frequencies are:

Gama – Gama registers at 40 Hz or higher. This is the latest brain frequency discovered by neuroscientists. Gama is referred as the active and yet relaxed frequency. Good examples are great athletes who are able to focus, concentrate, and perform under the stress of the pressure of the game or competition.

Beta – Beta is the most prevalent frequency in most humans. I refer to beta as the awakened, active, and stressed brain/mind state. It registers at 13 – 40 Hz. Good examples are very busy and active people who after performing their activity feel tired and exhausted.

Alpha – Alpha registers at 7 – 13 Hz. It is a relaxed, yet active state. In this state of relaxation, You are able to remain active, focused, concentrated, and energized most of the day while performing your required activities. Alpha also registers when you are resting or performing slower paced activities that are relaxing to you, and that when you perform them your mind is calm and at ease.

Theta – Theta registers at 4 – 7 Hz. It is referred as the state of deep rest and deep relaxation. It is also the state you achieve during deep meditation, and peaceful-dreaming sleep. This frequency is also referred as the hypnotic and self-healing state.

Delta – Delta registers at 4Hz, and is referred as deep dreamless sleep, and is the most regenerative brain state. In this state your body-mind-spirit can heal and regenerate itself. You can see why deep peaceful sleep every night is so essential to healthy living.

This section provides you with higher awareness of why relaxation and meditation are at the center of my Life Transformation Model. Through relaxation and meditation, you can easily and consistently remain in the three lower frequencies of your brain (Alpha, Theta, and Delta) most of the 24 hours of your day. This empowers you with the benefits of these three frequencies. You will be able to live a life in which you keep the effects of stress at bay while you live healthy, happy, long, and prosper. Operating at these frequencies allows you to also make the necessary changes within yourself much quicker so you can realize your dreams and desires.

This is the goal of all the processes I share with you in this book.

FROM BETA TO ALPHA, AND VOILÀ!
SHE PASSED HER TEST

After meeting with Klara for about thirty minutes, I told her she was doing all the right things to prepare. She only needed one thing: to reduce the anxiety she was feeling and her levels of stress. She replied, almost upset about what I was recommending, "This career is very stressful by nature, I would have to quit in order to reduce my anxiety and stress." I explained that she could still be very busy, but she did not have to be as anxious, stressed, tired, and frustrated. And besides, it was more than likely she would pass the test the next time she took it. With curiosity, she asked how she could do it.

BASIC FUNCTIONING OF THE BRAIN

I taught her two processes that day: **active relaxation** and **autogenic conditioning**. Two months later, she came to let me know that she had passed her test and was elated, but most of all she was still practicing the two interventions I had shared with her.

Relaxation and meditation are habits themselves. They need to be developed and become part of your life. Luckily, like Klara, they can be developed as you use them to make other changes and improvements you want to make in your life.

Why are relaxation and meditation the core lifestyle shift in The Life Transformation Paradigm model? Because consciously or subconsciously, people are seeking peace, sound health, and abundance for their life. Unfortunately, we think that we must reach them only through dedicated personal and professional effort or through force of the will.

We place so much importance on entertainment, vacationing, and all kinds of distractions, only to find out that they are also stressful events while we are living them or afterwards. How many times have you heard someone say, "I went here or did that and although it was fun, I am exhausted"? Another misconception is to work so hard, even to the point of getting sick, to become rich because of the belief that then we will be able to enjoy life without stress.

We have forgotten that stress is a state of the mind-body-spirit. In other words, stress is a perceived state. Two people can be exactly in the same circumstances and each can feel notably different levels of stress.

Stress is a perceived experience of the person that lives it. Thus, to be able to experience peace, good health, happiness, and abundance, which are perceptions also, people must improve their perception of the stress they go through in their lives. Stress will always interfere with your perception of other, more favorable conditions existing in your life.

The reason we need to live in a continuous state of relaxation and meditation is so that we can remain in a state of mind that is calm, cool, and collected, so as to be able to set aside misperceptions of the quality of our lives. It does not matter which level of socio-economic status you find yourself at or how bad you think your situation is. You must be able to remain calm, cool, and collected to be able to avoid the negative effects of stress in your life.

EVERYONE CAN BENEFIT FROM IMPROVING THEIR PERCEPTION OF STRESS

Deep inside, everyone desires peace, sound health, and happiness. Most people are running around trying to find them while in a state of stress, which is counterproductive. We do not realize that first we must find them within ourselves so they can be materialized without. Relaxation and meditation are the vehicles to reach them and experience them while we work at achieving success in all areas of our life.

I do not need to ask if or tell you that you are under a lot of stress. But you see, it is not the fact that you are under too much stress. It is how you are handling the stress that matters. I learned this lesson more than forty years ago. In this chapter, it is my mission to help you realize that while your stress levels are high, you do not have to suffer the consequences of it.

Living has become overly busy. We thought technology was going to make life easier and less hectic. However, the opposite has happened. As technology enters more into our lives, we look for more things to do. We are stressing and tiring our brains much more than ever before.

WHY ZEBRAS DON'T GET ULCERS

In addition to living a hectic life, we live through many psychological and social stressors which, over time and frequent repetitions, can wreak havoc on our health, peace, and happiness.

According to Robert M. Sapolsky, professor of biology and neurology at Stanford University and author of the book with the title of this section, animals are not concerned about issues such as relationship breakups, being fired or let go from a job, losing money in business, living with too much debt . . . you get the message.

What is worse, we bring on ourselves stressors in the name of responsibility, greater success, and even fun — stressors such as nervousness before a speech, being a caregiver, making more money or experiencing greater success in our careers, watching violent or terrifying movies, raising children to be good citizens, and on and on.

Please do not get me wrong. These activities are what make us human, but what makes them hazardous to our health is how we live through them. We find ourselves constantly stressed and perhaps even feeling tired or exhausted. What is disconcerting is the fact that too many people know and feel their levels of stress, but they get used to it, thinking this is the way to live.

Continuous exposure to high levels of stress has been associated with most illnesses. High blood pressure, heart problems, diabetes, depression, anxiety, eating disorders, digestive problems, and pain are but just a few examples of conditions that are associated with high stress levels.

Good health is necessary for a happy and peaceful existence. Good health is necessary to enjoy the good things in life, and to continue living a prosperous life. Good health is necessary to meet the high demands of life, and to be able to meet them successfully. This is the purpose of this book.

I have written it for you. You deserve to live a happy, peaceful, productive, and prosperous life in great health.

HOW STRESSED ARE YOU? EVALUATE YOUR LEVEL OF STRESS

Below is a stress perception test. Score yourself in each question per the instructions included. When you are done scoring each question, get a score for your test. The instructions for scoring it are also included.

This is a scientifically calibrated test. This makes your test score accurate. If you got a score of 12.5 or higher, your level of stress is abnormal. The higher the score, the more stress you have in your life. Everyone can benefit from reducing their levels of stress. Even if you score below 12.5, you too can get further benefits in health, peace, and well-being.

SELF-ASSESSMENT QUESTIONNAIRES

PERCEIVED STRESS SCALE

The questions in this scale ask you about your feelings and thoughts **during the last month**. In each case, you will be asked to indicate by circling **how often** you felt or thought a certain way.

Name: _____

Date: _____

Age: _____ Gender (Circle): M F Other: _____

0 = Never
1 = Almost Never
2 = Sometimes
3 = Fairly Often
4 = Very Often

1. In the last month, how often have you been upset because of something that happened unexpectedly? 0 1 2 3 4

2. In the last month, how often have you felt that you were unable to control the important things in your life? 0 1 2 3 4

3. In the last month, how often have you felt nervous and "stressed"? 0 1 2 3 4

4. In the last month, how often have you felt confident about your ability to handle your personal problems? 0 1 2 3 4

5. In the last month, how often have you felt that things were going your way? 0 1 2 3 4

6. In the last month, how often have you found that you could not cope with all the things that you had to do? 0 1 2 3 4

7. In the last month, how often have you been able to control irritations in your life? 0 1 2 3 4

8. In the last month, how often have you felt that you were on top of things? 0 1 2 3 4

9. In the last month, how often have you been angered because of things that were outside of your control? 0 1 2 3 4

10. In the last month, how often have you felt difficulties were piling up so high that you could not overcome them? 0 1 2 3 4

Mind Garden, Inc.
info@mindgarden.com
www.mindgarden.com

References

The PSS Scale is reprinted with permission of the American Sociological Association, from Cohen, S., Kamarck, T., and Mermelstein, R. (1983). "A global measure of perceived stress." *Journal of Health and Social Behavior, 24,* 386–396.

Cohen, S., and Williamson, G. "Perceived Stress in a Probability Sample of the United States." Spacapan, S., and Oskamp, S. (Eds.) *The Social Psychology of Health.* Newbury Park, CA: Sage, 1988.

Now score your stress inventory according to your answers. Here are the instructions:

First, reverse your answers to questions number 4, 5, 7, and 8. Look at each of these four questions and the number you circled originally. If you circled 0, then scratch out the 0 and circle the 4. If you circled 1, scratch out 1 and circle 3. If you circled 2, leave it unchanged. If you circled 3, scratch out 3 and circle 1. If you circled 4, scratch out 4 and circle 0. Once you have reversed these answers, then add up your circled answers from questions 1 through 10.

See the scored sample inventory on the next page. In this example the original selected answers are in italics font. The reversed answers for questions 4, 5, 7, and 8 are shown in bold, underlined text. The reversed answers are the numbers you add to the numbers you selected as answers to the rest of the questions to arrive at your total stress score.

PERCEIVED STRESS SCALE SCORING SAMPLE

The questions in this scale ask you about your feelings and thoughts **during the last month**. In each case, you will be asked to indicate by circling **how often** you felt or thought a certain way.

Name: _____

Date: _____

Age: _____ Gender (Circle): M F Other: _____

0 = Never
1 = Almost Never
2 = Sometimes
3 = Fairly Often
4 = Very Often

1. In the last month, how often have you been upset because of something that happened unexpectedly? 0 1 2 *3* 4

2. In the last month, how often have you felt that you were unable to control the important things in your life? 0 1 2 *3* 4

3. In the last month, how often have you felt nervous and "stressed"? 0 1 2 3 *4*

4. In the last month, how often have you felt confident about your ability to handle your personal problems? 0 *1* 2 **3** 4

5. In the last month, how often have you felt that things were going your way? 0 *1* 2 **3** 4

6. In the last month, how often have you found that you could not cope with all the things that you had to do? 0 1 2 *3* 4

7. In the last month, how often have you been able to control irritations in your life? 0 *1* 2 **3** 4

8. In the last month, how often have you felt that you were on top of things? *0* 1 2 3 **4**

9. In the last month, how often have you been angered because of things that were outside of your control? 0 1 2 *3* 4

10. In the last month, how often have you felt difficulties were piling up so high that you could not overcome them? 0 1 2 *3* 4

TOTAL STRESS SCORE = 32

INTERPRETATION OF THE SCORES

The Mind Garden perception stress survey (PSS) scoring has been normalized through a random survey sample of 2,387 respondents. Based on this sample, the stress level mean average for this survey is 12.8. What this means is that if your score is at or below the average of 12.8, you can consider yourself to have "normal" levels of stress and probably feel good most of the time. As your score gets above 12.8, you experience levels of stress out of the norm. This means that the higher it is above 12.8, the more you probably feel stressed, tired, and overloaded with responsibilities. You may even be experiencing frequent episodes of negative emotions such as frustration, lack of motivation, tiredness, impatience, and anger. You may feel exhausted, be experiencing health issues, or wondering if things will ever get better. However, stress management skills are helpful to everyone and even if your score is within the norm, this book will be of benefit to you. Lowering your levels of stress, regardless of the score, is good for everyone because it is always good to improve your physical, spiritual, and emotional health.

Now you have a better estimation of your stress levels. Although the results you got do not absolutely define your life, they point to how you feel about what is going on in your life. In the rest of this book, you will learn strategies to manage your life which will help you keep your levels of stress significantly lower than what is considered normal based on this test — and, most importantly, the improvements in your life will demonstrate it to you. More importantly, these strategies help everyone improve their quality of life, health, and longevity. They help people live productively regardless of the levels of stress they have in their lives.

You can live a happy, healthy, long, and prosperous life.

CHAPTER 3

Lifestyle Shift #1: Relaxation and Meditation—Peace Within Is Peace Without, Continued

Part 2: Being Relaxed Under Pressure and Stress Keeps You Healthy and Highly Productive

"The only workable strategy for maintaining productivity over the long run is to learn how to relax."

— Joan Borysenko, PhD, *Inner Peace for Busy People*

PEACE WITHIN IS PEACE WITHOUT

In the hurried and busy world of today, too many people are suffering from what I call "stress-itis." They spend a large portion of their day so immersed in their daily responsibilities, attempting to get them all met and satisfied responsibly, and at the end of the day they go home tired and exhausted, knowing that the following day the cycle will repeat itself.

Some will get even into greater stress. They will take on additional responsibilities, chasing a dream of making enough money or getting rich, all in the name of their family. They work themselves sick to make enough so they do not have to work so hard and be able to take vacations in a resort or a beach, living happily ever after. Do not get me wrong — these are all great desires and ideals, but more often than not, people will fail at these attempts and more than likely will end up with some sort of illness from the high levels of stress they put themselves under. Those who achieve the goal of getting rich find themselves working while on vacation, not being able to relax and enjoy it, which was initially the goal.

I know, I know — having money is not happiness, but it sure helps to get it. We have all heard this or a similar aphorism. I agree with pursuing higher goals, dreams, and ambitions. I am still doing this and I am, as of this writing, sixty-eight years old. But I am happy to tell you that I have been able to achieve all my dreams, goals, and desires, including financial freedom. However, with simple but intentional and consistent practices of relaxation and meditation, I have been able to achieve the life of peace, prosperity, and sound health I desired.

THE ART OF RELAXATION AND MEDITATION

Once I saw a sign that read, "Meditation is easy, you just need to do it." Meditation for healthy, happy, and abundant living requires that we relax and focus our attention on thoughts that are healthy and productive in nature or that we let any thought, sensation, or feeling out of our minds, and simply relax.

BENEFITS OF RELAXATION AND MEDITATION

The benefits of practicing relaxation and meditation are numerous. These benefits are documented in credible journals through scientific experiments.

Here are some benefits relaxation and meditation provide to your life:

- Increase energy and stamina;
- Increase longevity and promote healthier aging;
- Improve healthy sleep;

- Reduce oxidative stress;

- Oxygenate the brain and the blood stream;

- Contribute to the health and growth of neurons in the brain;

- Contribute to the decalcification of vessels;

- Improve blood circulation and pressure;

- Help improve body balance, coordination, and grounding;

- Improve memory, concentration, and comprehension;

- Contribute to the repair of cells at the molecular level;

- Increase mental, physical, and spiritual (emotional) health;

- Promote states of calmness, peace, and satisfaction with life; and

- Evoke the body/mind/spirit healing and wellness response.

Meditation is a state of being. Relaxation is the gateway to this state. Deep, relaxing breathing is the key.

LEARNING TO RELAX AND MEDITATE

Relaxing Breathing

The first technique we learn to empower ourselves to live in continuous relaxation and with minimal stress is relaxing breathing, also known as diaphragmatic breathing. Relaxing breathing is simple, and every form of meditation starts by teaching this technique. However, most meditation teachers teach it as part of your once or twice a day meditation practice or ritual. The way I teach the use of this technique is to use it all day, every day.

ACTIVE RELAXING BREATHING: BEING RELAXED WHEN BUSY OR UNDER PRESSURE

The next time you are waiting for a green light at a traffic light or driving in lots of traffic or facing a situation where you feel stressed, take a few seconds and practice active relaxing breathing. Look up for a few seconds and take three deep breaths, inhaling through your nose as much air as you can to fill your stomach, hold the air for a few seconds, and exhale freely through your mouth.

We should breathe like that as frequently as possible throughout the day. Active relaxing breathing, when practiced consistently, promotes better blood circulation, decompresses your vessels, oxygenates your entire body, improves brain processing, renews your energy levels, and keeps you at rest and peaceful.

Again, to take relaxing breaths, inhale slowly as much air as you can, bringing it into your stomach. Once you have filled your stomach with air, hold the air in for a count of four seconds and then release the air slowly through your nose or mouth, whichever is more comfortable to you. Repeat this cycle five or six times if you have the time available. This repetition, done five or six times, will take you about five minutes. Go ahead and try it right now if time allows.

Since you may not be used to breathing this way, feel free to take a normal breath between deep breaths. Eventually you will be able to breathe deeply more times in a row. Practice will make your breathing cycle longer, and you will be able to take more deep breaths continuously.

If you are in a hurry or busy, taking even one or two deep, relaxing breaths frequently will help you stay continuously relaxed. When you need to breathe deeply most is when you are busy and/or under pressure. At the beginning, you will need to remind yourself. As you get used to the practice, you will do it automatically all day long.

OTHER QUICK RELAXATION TECHNIQUES

Shoulder and Neck Massage with Deep, Relaxing Breathing

You can do this relaxation exercise anywhere, anytime you feel stressed out. Even if you feel all right, you can do it to promote a feeling of wellness and rest. You only need two to five minutes to do it.

Start massaging your left shoulder with your right hand and applying comfortable pressure. Massage your shoulder muscles all the way up to the right side of your neck. Take deep, relaxing breaths as you massage. Repeat the process on your right shoulder using your left hand.

Wave of Relaxation

The wave of relaxation is a quick relaxation technique, but it requires you to have quiet time by yourself. I have included this exercise here because it also serves as an introduction to meditation. You need at least five minutes of quiet time by yourself; however, you can take longer for a deeper relaxation and stress reduction effect.

1. Sit or lie down comfortably and begin taking deep, relaxing breaths. With each deep breath, scan your body and notice what parts of your body may be feeling tense or in pain.

2. Take a deep breath and, when you exhale, imagine the entire feeling of relaxation going to those parts of your body that are tense or in pain.

3. When you send the feeling of relaxation, you can send it to a specific part or to all parts at once. You can send the wave of relaxation to your entire body if you prefer.

LEARNING TO MEDITATE

There are many types of meditation because the practice has its origins in many different spiritual beliefs. However, once you understand the practice, you discover that it is all about attention, concentration, and purpose or intention in a state of deep relaxation. One thing about the mind/brain is that for it to work at utmost efficiency, it helps for it to be in a relaxed state. Many scientific studies using biofeedback, and now PET scans and MRIs, have demonstrated that when the brain is in a state of meditation, it can learn faster, the body can heal itself faster, and creativity and problem-solving abilities are improved. Studies have even demonstrated that the brain is capable of regenerating itself when meditation is practiced consistently. For the purposes of this book, the greatest benefits are the natural state of peace and stressless productivity and health improvements.

Meditation is not a complicated process. It is, however, a habit to be developed. Most people want to improve their lives, but developing the habits required to do it is where most fail. However, if you are willing to try and do it, meditation is an easy habit to develop because of the immediate benefits it brings to you. As you experience the benefits, you feel self-motivated to continue practicing. That is what happened to John. Below I share his testimony with you:

John was referred to me by his mom. She and I worked together for over twenty-five years as college counselors. She knew about my work and sent John my way. John had graduated as a teacher just about a year ago. He had attempted the teacher certification test four times before and had failed it. He was working as a teacher in probationary status pending passing his certification test.

John came to me in a high state of anxiety because if he did not pass the test in the next attempt, he would lose his job and could never work as a teacher in the state of Texas. I met with John three times and taught him relaxing breathing plus two other meditations to help him get his self-confidence back and help his memory work better during the test. Here is what John shared with me a month later, after passing the state test:

"First off, I just want to say how thankful I am for reaching out and getting the help I didn't know I needed from you, Dr. Baltazar. After numerous attempts at taking and not passing my teaching certification exam, I did not know what else to do considering I had studied nearly all the study guides known to man. It was then that I was able to reach out to Dr. Baltazar and explain to him my situation, and where I was in my own head when it came to this exam. He explained to me what was going on and had me taking a bit of a different approach to taking the exam. At first, like with anything out of the ordinary, I was a bit skeptical, but I went ahead and began to do the meditation exercises he advised me to do with an open mind. It was then that I felt a shift in my confidence and my outlook on the exam itself. As I continued to meet with Dr. Baltazar my confidence also continued to grow. Before I knew it, my testing date was here and rather than being nervous as I was EVERY other time I had taken it, I was able to walk into the testing room knowing that I was going to pass it. Dr. Baltazar was able to help me find and gain the confidence I had lost in myself and my ability to pass the exam, I can gladly say that I was able to pass my exam and have not lost the confidence that he taught me to have in not only the things I am doing but to have the confidence in myself. I owe Dr. B the world, without him and his guidance I have no idea where I would be or if I would even be able to call myself a teacher. THANK YOU FOR EVERYTHING, DR. B. you were/are the ultimate game changer."

Meditation works, and it works to improve all areas of your life.

DEVELOPING THE HABIT AND SKILL OF MEDITATION

To develop this habit, start with simple and short relaxation and meditation sessions. Here are some simple ways to learn to focus the mind, be present, and reduce stress. Take five minutes to perform any one of these activities at least twice per day. It is even better if you make time to practice more times per day:

- Focus your attention on an object as you relax with deep, relaxing breaths, and think thoughts only related to the object you are observing.

- When you are eating anything, breathe deeply as you focus your attention on the food and your act of eating.

- Find alone time and simply breathe deeply and slowly, relax your body, and let go of any thoughts that come to your mind by focusing your attention on your breathing and feelings of relaxation.

- Relax and focus your attention on a positive word or affirmation and the meaning and thoughts the word or affirmation brings to your mind.

- Relax and think about the positive characteristics of someone you love.

- Practice deep relaxing breathing meditations for five minutes at a time and gradually increase them by five minutes until you can stay in meditation for a full twenty-minute session.

SLOWLY BUT SURELY — THE FOUNDATION MUST BE LAID DOWN FIRST

Do not worry if at first you cannot remain in meditation for a long time. Start your practice in small segments of time. At first, it is most important to focus on the practice of breathing and relaxing. You will learn to meditate gradually as you continue reading and doing the practices or exercises in each lifestyle shift covered in this book.

Your Practice Assignment

1. Practice taking deep, relaxing breaths throughout the day, every day.

2. Practice some of the focusing techniques from the section "Developing The Habit and Skill of Meditation" in this chapter.

3. Practice deep relaxing breathing meditations twice a day. Find a quiet space wherever you are and start doing them for five minutes, and gradually increase them until you can stay in meditation for sessions of twenty minutes.

4. Practice the other quick relaxation techniques included in this chapter.

You do not have to do all the practices, but the more you do the better. These practices will help you get used to being still, quiet, and relaxed, and prepare you for the implementation of the other six shifts in your life. The main vehicle for implementing and living each life transformation shift is meditation and relaxation. Specific meditations are recommended in each chapter to make change easier and faster. You are just beginning the transformation of your life into one of peace, happiness, longevity, and prosperity.

THERE IS ALWAYS ROOM
TO GROW

Everybody, including me and you, can be better.
Everybody, including me and you, can improve.
Name the subject; there's always room to grow.
This is the difference between mediocrity and success.
It is a truth that only a few people really know.

Whatever you do, you can always try to do it better.
This is the difference between average and excellent.
Most settle for average and prevent themselves
from getting the reward.
It is sad but true that only a few seek to improve.
They do not know that with improvement, life gives more.

Keep an open mind when something new is offered.
Do not ignore it or reject it prematurely.
If it is to help you and it is for good, try it.
Explore it. Make the time for it.
For your success, this could be a valuable tool.

Everybody wants to do better in life.
It does not matter at what level they are at.
Most do not put in the extra effort,
and only live in Wonderland.
Now ask yourself: are you going to live like that?

— Dr. Jose M. Baltazar

CHAPTER 4

Lifestyle Shift #2: Faith and Self-Belief— The Only Limits Are Those We Place on Ourselves

Something I learned in my studies of the mind in the field of mind-body medicine and in accelerated learning psychology was the scientific truth to the psychological principle that the human being has unlimited potential. What has been able to demonstrate this and prove it as a fact are studies on the brain to find out how it works. Our brain is a magnificent creation. A magnificent organ. And every single human being has one of these, and in its own way, for each human being, this organ is unlimited. It is your brain that makes you limitless and capable of doing anything you set yourself to do.

LIVING BY FAITH AND SELF-BELIEF, NOT BY SIGHT

Faith and self-belief is the second component in the Life Transformation Paradigm Faith means belief, trust, certainty, conviction, assurance, and expectation.

My father taught me many positive values and beliefs. I remember two that I believe have helped me navigate through life successfully. One was "God always provides, God never abandons us." The second was "To prosper, you first need to change yourself. You have to become a better person."

My father was not a millionaire, nor was he a highly educated individual. He was an entrepreneur and small business owner and spent most of his life in hard labor. However, he was always able to save, stay out of debt, succeed in his small ventures, and provide abundantly for his family.

Whenever he started one of his ventures, he did it trusting with certainty that it would work out — and work out it did. I remember him stating frequently to himself and others his phrase: "God always provides, God never abandons us." This belief took him to different ventures (grocery stores, toy buying and reselling, independent trucking), all of them successful. Faith of this type, one that looks to a future desired outcome with certainty and expectation, is requisite for achieving higher desires and goals in any area of our lives.

YOU ARE ALREADY LIVING BY FAITH AND SELF-BELIEF

Most people struggle to pursue their dreams, and if they decide to pursue higher and bigger dreams and desires, they usually fail because they do not first improve themselves in faith and self-belief. Your everyday faith and self-belief will only take you to a certain point or level in life. To reach your higher desires, you need to develop greater faith and self-belief than the ones that have brought you to where you are right now.

Everyone lives life in faith and self-belief. It is the level of faith and self-belief that determines how much we can accomplish in life.

I remember Jesse. He was working as a human resources associate for a company. He had his master's degree and was performing the job of a human resources director at a much lower salary because he did not have his certification as a human resources professional. I met him in my accelerated learning class. He shared with me that this was the reason for taking my course. He had attempted to pass the certification test and had not been able to pass it. He completed my class, and a month later he wrote me a note thanking me. He had passed the test and shared that the lessons that helped him most were the ones in faith and self-confidence. Once he believed again with conviction (faith) that he had the intelligence and knowledge to pass the test (self-belief), he had been able to pass it with a higher score than the minimum.

WHAT IS FAITH?

People who are not living the life they desire to live are being held back by weak faith. Faith is an important teaching in most religious philosophies. For example, faith is defined in the Bible as "The assurance of things hoped for, the conviction of things not seen" (Hebrews 11:1); the Bhagavad Gita, the timeless scripture of India, teaches in Gita 17:28 (explained by Paramahansa Yogananda) that one should abandon as early as possible the absurd tendency of the doubting mind which, sitting on the riverbank and fearful of plunging into the water, says, "Yes, but how can I be sure I won't drown?"

Faith is belief with conviction, assurance, certainty, and trust. All of us live life by faith, and this is demonstrated every minute of our existence. Even the next minute of our life is not guaranteed. Even if it crosses our minds whether we are going to live through it or not, most of us are certain we will be alive after sixty seconds have gone by. We go about our daily life trusting and assured that events and activities that happen routinely in our lives will occur again. We get up and get ready for work. We drive to work and perform our daily duties. Every single day of our life is an act of faith. We believe the cycle of living will repeat again, and we trust it will happen because experience assures us it will. Our degree of certainty for most of us is almost, if not completely, 100 percent.

It is this high degree of certainty about daily life that can also keep most people from venturing into new or unfamiliar experiences and prevents them from attaining more ambitious goals and desires. Deep down inside, they know taking the risks involved in achieving greater dreams would make them happier and more fulfilled; however, they struggle with the uncertainty inherent in the future. This is the logic behind the biblical statement, "For to everyone who has, more will be given, and he will have an abundance; but from the one who does not have, even what he does have shall be taken away" (Matthew 25:29, NASB). Everything is available to all of us, but not all of us have the level of faith necessary to pursue our highest desires. Our faith needs to increase. Because we always live in the present and look toward the future, our faith must increase in order for our lives to increase and prosper. Later in this chapter I will teach you some basic but powerful techniques to increase your faith. Let us talk about self-belief first.

SELF-BELIEF

I just saw a phrase that reads: "I am certain we are here for a greater purpose than to get up, go to work, pay bills, retire, and die." This is true wisdom, and most people know it, but the reality is different. Most people live a life better than the one depicted by this post, but also most people are not living the life they want or desire.

Ask yourself the question: is there something in my life that I would like to realize but have not mastered the motivation and courage to start working towards it, or do I keep coming up with reasons as to why it is too hard or not possible — or even worse, have I resigned myself and convinced myself that it is not for me? If you answered "yes" to any part of this question, you are not living the life you want and that you are designed to live.

A friend asked me, "You have faith and self-belief in the same spot in your Life Transformation Paradigm. Is it because they mean the same thing, or is there a difference?" My answer: they go together but they are not the same, exactly. Faith is the state you are in, and self-belief determines the level of faith you have.

What determines the level of self-belief you have? Answer: your present beliefs determine your level of faith. Beliefs are filters in your mind through which you screen and process all the information you receive from your environment. Your beliefs drive your behavior. You always behave consistently with your beliefs. You cannot get beyond your own beliefs unless you consciously decide to improve them.

By nature, we humans desire better and higher things for our lives, but we tend to hold strongly to the beliefs we have developed. Unfortunately, many of those beliefs are false and limit our faith. To grow, prosper, and live happier lives, we need to grow in faith, and to grow in faith we must reinforce the true beliefs we have, and we must abandon false and limiting beliefs.

Our family came to the United States in 1967. For the first few years, I remember my mom telling herself and others frequently that she wished she could speak English. Whenever I told her to go ahead and take classes, she had many reasons (limiting beliefs) why she could not do it. "I'm too old." "I did not go to school enough years when I was younger." "I am too busy at home." "You can interpret for me." And many other reasons. Eventually she stopped expressing her desire and stopped thinking about it — or, since she was not doing anything to learn the language, stopped talking about it and learned to live without it. My mom was a great mom to us and had it not been for her limiting beliefs, she could have also become more self-empowered by learning English. She never realized her heart's desire to learn English. I believe she knew she could have been a much more self-realized and self-empowered person if she had learned the English language.

Every one of us is designed to follow our dreams and desires and bring them to reality. This is one of the foundations of living a happy and fulfilled life.

HOW TO INCREASE IN FAITH AND SELF-BELIEF

One of the first interventions most personal change professionals use to help people get what they want is called "changing beliefs." We start with this process because in most cases, what keeps people from getting ahead in life is their current belief system. The general belief on the part of coaches and psychologists is that helping people change their beliefs will pull them forward and get them unstuck because they believe more in themselves and thus become more self-motivated.

Changing beliefs works, but is not a complete solution. If it were, more people would accomplish their goals, dreams, and desires, and would live happy and fulfilling lives, yet most people still do not accomplish them and, according to statistics, more and more people live unhappy and unfulfilled lives. Changing beliefs is only one half of the process. The other half of the process is faith.

Faith is more transcending and spiritual. Faith is certainty that there is a power stronger than our own. It is that power that everyone looks to when something major disrupts our existence — events like 9/11 or school or shopping center shootings. At the individual level, we look to this higher power, which most in the Western world call God, when something deeply hurtful happens to us. People who lack faith ask themselves why bad things happen to them and feel desperate, and many fall into anxiety, depression, and/or suicide. To complete the process of increasing in self-belief, we must also increase our faith.

INCREASING IN FAITH

When I work with clients, I approach the topic from their own perspective and belief system:

1. If they are Christian, I approach it from biblical teachings.

2. If they are from a different system of spiritual beliefs, I approach it from their own belief system. They just need to tell me about it, and the interventions can be tailored to their belief system.

3. If they do not practice or believe in any spiritual system, I approach it from the area of emotional states. Everyone experiences emotions. How we feel at any one time reflects our spiritual state. When we are in a positive emotional state or mood,

then our spiritual state is positive; therefore, our faith is prone to being stronger. If we are in a negative emotional state or mood, our spirit is in a negative state or mood and, therefore, our faith is more prone to being weaker.

Whichever option from these three you find yourself in, increasing your faith is possible and not difficult. One thing to be aware of is that increasing in faith is a lifelong process and, therefore, it requires constant work. As you grow in faith, life becomes easier and more fulfilling because you learn to be in a state of faith more consistently, regardless of what happens in your life and the life of others. Another interesting fact is that the more consistently you live in a state of faith, the more positive things happen to you. It is amazing and true!

PRACTICES TO GROW IN FAITH AND SELF-BELIEF

Remember that faith is believing with certainty in the outcomes you desire. Remember also that we live life already in a state of faith. Every single routine action you take every single day where you do not question the outcome, you do it believing with certainty that you will be successful. Imagine if every time you got in the shower, you did it thinking, "What if I fall? What if I break a leg and it won't heal? What if I fall and hit my head?" and so on and so on. You would probably not shower at all, and if you did, you would probably do it in so much fear that you would cause what you had been fearing to happen.

We have developed this level of faith through repeated experience and seeing the desired outcome repeatedly. These repeated experiences and successful outcomes exist in our subconscious. We perform these actions without thinking or questioning them, trusting and feeling certain that we will get the desired results. This is the state of faith that we need to have when we attempt something new or more ambitious. We need to feel certain and trust that we will get the desired results even before we attempt the actions to get it. This is faith.

Here are three effective ways to grow in faith to improve any area of your life you wish to.

USING YOUR CURRENT FAITH TO
SPRING UP TO HIGHER FAITH

You already have experienced success. You have achieved many things already. This means you acted with faith to get these successes. Even if you felt some uncertainty, you went ahead and hoped and trusted that you would get the desired outcomes. In this meditation exercise, you will use a successful experience you have had to increase your level of faith, belief, and trust that you can be successful again at getting something you desire for your better future. Through repeated practice of this exercise, you can implant greater faith, belief, and trust in your mind permanently and make it a subconscious automatic process.

1. Find a quiet space where you can be by yourself for at least thirty minutes and have pen and paper ready.

2. Sit comfortably and relax for about five minutes, taking slow, deep breaths just like we learned in Chapter 3.

3. Identify a previous success you have achieved in your life that gave you a sense of happiness and fulfillment. With your eyes closed, spend five minutes contemplating your successful experience, getting in touch with the feelings you felt back then. Keep these feelings and positive sensations in the front of your mind; open your eyes and continue with the next step.

4. Write down what you want to bring into your life, and below it, write as many reasons as possible why you want this in your life. What benefits will it bring to your life?

5. Take a few deep breaths and remain relaxed.

6. Read your statement slowly and take a few minutes to contemplate it, and — with your eyes closed — visualize yourself having

achieved your desire and enjoying the benefits you expect. As you visualize it, get in touch with your feelings about it. Enjoy the imagery for about five minutes.

7. Keeping the positive images, thoughts, and feelings of your future successful experience in your mind, take a few deep, relaxing breaths and open your eyes.

To plant the certainty of future success in your mind permanently, repeat this process at least once per day for the next ten days or twice per day for one week.

MEDITATION TO INCREASE YOUR SPIRITUAL FAITH

Choose the one statement below which resonates with you.

> "Therefore I tell you, all that you ask for in prayer, believe that you will receive it and it shall be yours." (Mark 11:24, NABRE)

> There is a greater creative power that permeates and oversees the entire universe. This power is within me also. My being reflects and contains this power; therefore, I also have the power to oversee my own life and create in it what is best for me and those I love.

> My emotions reflect my spiritual state and my level of faith. I know that by remaining hopeful and optimistic despite my circumstances, I demonstrate my attitude of certainty that what I desire is already on its way to me.

1. As the words speak to you, contemplate what message you get. What are they telling you? When you get a message, do not question it. Simply listen and accept the message you get and

continue thinking about it, focusing only on the message you are getting.

2. If at first the phrase does not speak to you, simply read the phrase slowly a few more times, leaving a gap of time between readings, and see if the words speak to you as you continue to reread it.

3. Continue the processes of relaxing breathing, reading, and contemplating for a period of ten to twenty minutes.

Do this type of meditation frequently. Faith is a state of mind. It is a way of thinking about living life. Meditation allows us to think deeply and to place new thoughts in our mind in a more potent way than other forms of therapy or mind conditioning. The foundation and center piece of my Life Transformation Paradigm is relaxation and meditation. Relaxation opens the door to peace. Meditation is the way to get peace. Relaxation and meditation are the foundations to live the life you are designed to live: healthy, happy, long, prosperous, and without stress.

MEDITATION TO BE CERTAIN OF YOUR DESIRES

Frequently, people who want to take larger steps to improve their lives hesitate because they are not certain if they should pursue their desires. They doubt themselves and waste time wondering if they should try. They question themselves so much that they end up convincing themselves to continue their life the way it is.

Any desire that is for your benefit and those you love is meant to be pursued, especially if it keeps coming frequently to your mind. Desires that come to your mind repeatedly have the power to become reality. People intuitively know what will fulfill them more, but due to their limiting beliefs and therefore their limited faith, most give up their greater desires and squelch their minds and hearts and prevent themselves from living a more fulfilling life.

The meditation below helps you identify and be certain about those desires you need to pursue.

1. Go to your private and quiet place and lie down flat, fully stretched out and facing upward, or sit comfortably on a chair with your back straight. Close your eyes and begin taking deep, relaxing breaths. Allow your body to relax and continue taking deep, relaxing breaths throughout the meditation.

2. Close your eyes and, as you get relaxed, bring to your mind a desire you have.

3. Continue relaxing and, as you contemplate what you want, ask yourself or notice if this desire has come to your mind a few times.

4. As you get more relaxed, ask yourself if this is something you really want in your life.

5. Keep relaxing and see what answer you get. If the answer is "yes," accept it and let the answer be in your heart and mind.

6. If the answer is "no" or there is some doubt, then you should not pursue it, at least not right now.

7. Exit the meditation by opening your eyes and taking a few more relaxing breaths.

8. Trust your own heart and spirit, and if you believe in God, trust him the most. In the state of meditation, you receive the answers you need for your life to be at its best. Faith says, "Anything is possible." Self-belief says, "I can do anything. I have the power and the resources to do it."

Let us work on your self-belief.

MEDITATIONS TO STRENGTHEN YOUR SELF-BELIEF

Once you check the validity of your dreams and desires, you need to strengthen your own belief in yourself to empower yourself and ensure that you get them. The three meditations that follow will help you with that process.

MEDITATIVE AFFIRMATIONS

Everyone who works in the field of self-empowerment and self-improvement recommends affirmations to help ourselves in improving our self-esteem and self-belief. Louise Hay, in her book *You Can Heal Your Life,* states, "Every thought we think is creating our future." Therefore, to create a better future for ourselves, we need to start by improving our thinking about ourselves.

My approach to working with affirmations is by repeating them in the state of meditation. The mind accepts the meaning of affirmations much easier and translates it to behaviors much quicker. Change and improvement occurs much easier and faster when done in a slower brain wave (see Chapter 2, "Five Basic Brain Wave Frequencies"). How deeply you can relax determines the type of brain wave you are functioning in. I can assure you that when you relax for five to ten minutes initially, you will reach the alpha brain wave, and with practice you can reach the delta or theta brain wave in ten to twenty minutes.

RELAXATION RESPONSE MEDITATION

This type of meditation was developed by Dr. Herbert Benson of the Harvard University Medical Center, and although it is used mainly for wellness and healing, it also works for changing thinking and behaviors.

This meditation requires that you think of a single word that triggers thoughts, images, and emotions about the change you want to make. The affirmation can also be a short phrase that has the same effect in your mind. You can develop your own affirmation with wording that you prefer.

Short phrases should be written in the present tense, like the examples below. The phrases need to personally speak to you and be stated in the present tense, and you can write them specifically for the behavior you want to improve or develop.

For the purposes of this exercise, please choose the affirmation that you can best associate with from the three that follow. (You can think about the specific changes you want as you repeat the phrase.)

Every day, in every way, I am better and better.

I am made in the image of God; therefore, I have all the qualities of God in me.

I have all the abilities and power to realize my desires.

1. Go to your private and quiet place and lie down flat, fully stretched out and facing upward, or sit comfortably on a chair with your back straight. Close your eyes and begin taking deep, relaxing breaths. Allow your body to relax and continue taking deep, relaxing breaths throughout the meditation.

2. Close your eyes and, as you get relaxed, bring to your mind or read the affirmation you chose. Read it slowly and feel what the affirmation means to you.

3. Continue relaxing and repeating the affirmation slowly for at least ten minutes.

4. Let thirty seconds to one minute lapse between each time you read the phrase to visualize and feel the changes you want to make, and how they will manifest in your life.

5. When the ten or twenty minutes are over, open your eyes slowly and exit the meditation by stretching and breathing deeply for a few minutes.

Practice this meditation for seven to ten days and notice how your thinking improves about yourself. Your behavior will also reflect the changes in your thinking. You will surprise yourself.

GETTING LEVERAGE MEDITATION

Getting leverage is a procedure that helps you realize your own capabilities to achieve anything you desire. You use past desires or goals you have realized that, when you achieved them, they gave you a sense of happiness and greater self-empowerment and self-esteem. The getting leverage process is based on the truth that all individuals have been successful in the past, but they tend to forget their successes over time or do not give themselves the credit they deserve anymore. Once people accept and appreciate their past successes again, they learn to trust themselves again, and trust their ability to achieve new and higher aspirations.

1. Find a quiet space where you can be by yourself for at least thirty minutes and have a pen and paper ready.

2. Sit comfortably and relax for about five minutes, taking slow, deep breaths just as we learned in Chapter 3.

3. Identify a previous success in your life that gives you a sense of happiness, fulfillment, and empowerment. The success you identify does not have to be something super-outstanding. It just needs to be an experience significant to you that at one point in your life you were committed to and resolute about achieving, and that when you remember it in getting ready for this exercise, you realize at one point that it was a goal that you desired to achieve, and you did.

4. Once you identify your successful experience, with your eyes closed, spend five to ten minutes contemplating your successful experience, getting in touch again with the feelings you felt back then. Keep these feelings and positive sensations in your heart and mind and continue relaxing as you relive your successful experience in your mind.

5. Talk to yourself positively and affirmatively as you re-experience your success in your own language, i.e., "If I was able to realize this past desire, I can do it again. I have what it takes to do it. It was not easy, but I stuck to it and I did it. I should not hesitate nor doubt. I will be successful in this new goal I've set for myself."

6. Keeping the positive feelings and thoughts of your past successful experience in your mind and heart, take a few deep, relaxing breaths and open your eyes.

To continue building up your self-belief and self-confidence, repeat this process at least once per day for the next ten days or twice per day for one week.

YOUR CIRCLE OF SUCCESS MEDITATION

The circle of success is an imagery meditation combined with deep relaxation to slow your brain waves down to the theta level. This deeper level of relaxation allows your subconscious to accept information contained in the imagery much more readily and encourages behavior modification — in this case, self-belief and self-motivation — to happen at a faster rate.

This meditation exercise is broken up into two steps, each with a series of steps:

Step 1: Visualize Yourself Being Successful

1. Take a few deep breaths to relax and feel peace within yourself.

2. Remain relaxed by breathing deeply and slowly. Identify the goal or desire you want to accomplish and describe it in writing or draw a picture of it representing how your life will look once that desire is a reality in your life. Write or draw as many benefits as possible that it will bring to your life.

3. Spend five to ten minutes looking at your picture or reading your description of your vision for the desire you want to bring into your life. As you do this, allow yourself to imagine living your life with your goal already realized.

Step 2: Experience Your Circle of Excellence

1. Stay relaxed. Keep taking deep, relaxing breaths.

2. Stand up in a floor space where there is free space in front of you big enough for you to be able to imagine a circle on the floor about four or five feet in diameter in front of you.

3. Place on the floor, in the center of the imaginary circle, your picture or your written description of how you imagine your life

with your desire or goal already being real. Leave your picture or writing on the floor and step out of the circle.

4. Now close your eyes and imagine the circle in front of you and your picture in the middle of it. You are standing just outside the circle; now imagine, in your visualization, that the entire circle turns bright, including your picture or description in the middle of it. The circle has become a circle of bright, shining, pure, and peaceful light.

5. As you look at the bright, peaceful circle, go ahead and take five slow, deep, relaxing breaths. Once you feel relaxed:

   a. Slowly step into the circle and step over your picture of your vision. Continue to relax by breathing deeply and slowly.

   b. Imagine your vision already being a reality and let your mind and your body become filled with your positive vision and the positive feelings that come to you with that reality. Give yourself enough time to imagine your positive future and feel the positive feelings it creates within you.

   c. Take one more deep breath and open your eyes, and slowly step back out of the circle. As you step out of the circle, bring with you your mental vision and the emotions you felt.

   d. Now pick up the paper of your vision and your shining imaginary circle. Fold your picture and your shining circle and put them in one of your pockets or in your purse, or hold them in your hand and put them away later.

   e. Once you have done this, sit down and remain relaxed for five to ten minutes. Then open your eyes, stand up, and stretch to re-energize yourself.

   f. The reason for carrying your vision and your circle of success in your purse or pocket is to have them available for practice and to carry the experience with you all the time.

When this exercise is performed in a meditative state, the feelings of competence, self-confidence, and self-motivation increase almost immediately after the first experience with the exercise. However, some individuals may need more repetitions of the process. Once the imagery is clear in your mind and you experience emotions more vividly, you will experience the increased self-belief and self-confidence within you. You will feel empowered to act and to succeed.

> "What we think about ourselves becomes the truth for ourselves."
>
> — Louise Hay

FAITH

Faith is an attitude, a value, and a virtue.
Faith is a human quality that demands belief.
Faith demands a commitment to a dream.
Faith requires living beyond comfort and relief.

Faith is a conviction of what we cannot see.
Faith is expecting better times for you and me.
Faith is not concerned with just what's visible.
Faith can see and feel what is still invisible.

Faith is not material. It's of the spirit.
Faith is a frame of mind and spirit.
Faith grows when you believe beyond what's touchable.
Faith grows when you believe in what seems impossible.

Faith lifts us up when we're down.
Faith helps us get up and keep trying.
Faith helps us see beyond pain and sorrow.
Faith helps us believe in a better tomorrow.

Faith moves us to seek and expect the best.
Faith reassures us that we are worthy.
Faith builds up our self-esteem.
Faith reassures us that we too can realize our dreams.

— Dr. Jose M. Baltazar

SELF-BELIEF

There are two ways you can live your life.
One gets you ahead. The other serves just to survive.
One encourages trying and take new risks.
The other holds you back and keeps you in a freeze.

One way knows improvement is not easy,
but it knows It is worth the try.
The other makes you doubtful,
and only leaves you dreaming in your cry.

One makes you feel worthwhile
and gets you what you want.
The other leaves you disappointed
and always saying that you can't.

So which way do you prefer,
the way of self-doubt and failure,
or the way of self-confidence and faith?
The first keeps you frustrated and unhappy.
The second encourages you to try
and always do the best you can.

— Dr. Jose M. Baltazar

CHAPTER 5

Lifestyle Shift #3: Vision—Activate the Law of Attraction

"Vision is the result of dreams in action."

— Joel Barker, futurist,
The Power of Vision training course (1990)

PERSONAL VISION: THE FOUNDATION TO REALIZE ALL THAT YOU WANT

Vision is a well-known concept in organizational psychology and leadership psychology. We call successful leaders visionaries, and we refer to successful companies as having a clear vision driven by a strong purpose and mission. Joel Barker states that research demonstrates that vision is not the only ingredient needed for a successful future, but it is the most important one — not only for companies and nations, but also for individuals.

As individual beings, we need to improve this self-leadership quality within each of us to experience continuous improved and long-lasting success. People need to have knowledge of and practice the principle of vision if they are to achieve and live their higher desires and dreams. These are natural and innate longings in every human being. We need to continuously empower ourselves. The Life Transformation Paradigm lifestyle, when applied as a systemic and holistic approach to living life, fulfills these innate desires in the human being.

I worked with a young man whose name is George. He came to me because he was told I worked with people who had trouble controlling their anger. When I started working with him, he told me his main concern was losing his girlfriend. He was already living with her, and they had been making plans to get married. However, lately they had been frequently getting into arguments and the arguments had escalated to the brink of violence on his part, and his girlfriend was threatening to leave him.

When George first came to my office, he had a grim look on his face that, as he started telling me about his situation, changed to deep worry, coupled with a trembling voice and shallow breathing. This was our first session, and I quickly asked him to do a ten-minute relaxation meditation together with me. I guided him through the meditation, teaching him in the process how to breathe deeply to release tension. After ending the meditation, I also trained him on how to remain relaxed throughout the day by using my active deep breathing technique, and how to use it whenever he sensed that an argument was about to start with his girlfriend or any other instance triggered his anger.

After I gathered some more background information about his life and his relationship with his girlfriend, I made an appointment with George for the following week. I gave him the assignment of practicing the ten-minute relaxing breathing meditation at least once a day and practicing active deep breathing throughout each day until we met again.

George showed up the following week and when he came in, he was smiling and looked relaxed, refreshed, and full of energy. I invited him to sit down and asked him how his week had gone. He proceeded in a state of excitement to relate his experiences with his girlfriend. He explained that he had been able to avoid getting into arguments that would have triggered his anger before by simply taking deep breaths and telling himself "relax,

relax, relax" and allowing his girlfriend to say what she wanted to say, even in a loud voice. This demonstrates to you why, in my Life Transformation Paradigm, relaxation and meditation become the center for living life.

As George continued to share with me his amazement at being able to hold his anger down by his practice of deep breathing and relaxation, he asked the question: "Is that all there is to it? I mean, my girlfriend is kind of surprised and glad that I have not blown up with anger like before, and I feel excited at my ability to hold my anger off, but I think both of us wonder how to talk about the issues about which we get angry. It is like what do we do now? What if we eventually can't control our anger if we continue talking about the issue that caused the argument?"

"You obviously want more from the relationship than just to prevent getting angry, am I right, George?"

He replied, "Yes, I love my girlfriend and want to marry her, but I also want to be able to discuss and resolve issues and disagreements peacefully, not just avoid getting angry. I want a happy marriage."

Notice what George is saying. A happy marriage is a greater vision than the original vision he came to me with of controlling his anger. George needed to develop and focus on his vision, not just on the immediate need to control his anger.

VISION GIVES YOU PURPOSE FOR LIVING

In his seminal book *Man's Search for Meaning*, Dr. Victor Frankl, the renowned psychotherapist, narrates his own experience of survival and that of other survivors of Nazi concentration camps. In his research, he discovered that most people who survived had a vision of what they would do once they were out of the camps. He writes:

> "Any attempt at fighting the camp's psychopathological influence on the prisoners by psychotherapeutic or psycho-hygienic methods

had to aim at giving them strength by pointing out to them a future goal to which they could look forward. Instinctively some prisoners attempted to find one on their own. It is a peculiarity of man that he can only live by looking to the future. And this is his salvation in the most difficult moments of his existence, although he sometimes has to force his mind to the task."

VISION — ALL ACHIEVEMENTS BEGIN IN THE MIND

Vision is the third component of the Life Transformation Paradigm. So far, you have learned the first two shifts to make in your lifestyle: one, you know how to live relaxed and in a state of rest and peace by integrating a consistent practice of continuous and daily relaxation and meditation. Two, you also have learned how to live a life which consistently grows in faith and self-belief. These two lifestyle shifts bring peace, tranquility, and assurance to your life.

The third shift, vision, helps you materialize all your future dreams and desires. You will live a life of hope, optimism, certainty, self-realization, continuous progress, and growth. When you practice the first three lifestyle shifts — relaxation and meditation, faith and self-belief, and vision — you will turn your desires, dreams, and goals into reality with greater certainty, expectation, and speed. The more consistent and stronger each of these factors is, the faster your desire becomes reality. For as long as you keep up your continuous growth in each of these factors, whatever desire or goal you decide you want to bring into your life will be yours.

As Dr. Frankl says, we can live only by looking to the future, and looking to the future is our salvation when we face difficult circumstances, even though at times we must force ourselves to find a reason for looking to our future. Here is where vision becomes essential. This is how big achievements in history have materialized. From Einstein's theory of relativity to President Kennedy's getting to the moon, from the founding of the United States to Dr. Martin Luther King's civil rights movement, vision has been the greatest motivator. Those who hold on relentlessly to their vision continue pursuing it despite problems and obstacles.

SOMETIMES WE MUST FORCE OUR MIND TO THE TASK OF FINDING A REASON TO LOOK TO THE FUTURE

Vision is always in action within us. We already intuitively know how vision works; otherwise, we would not be where we are today. However, there is a point in most peoples' lives where they start wishing instead of envisioning. There are four main reasons why people become resigned to their circumstances although inside they desire to become and achieve more. They become resigned because:

1. Their higher aspirations and desires seem much more difficult to achieve than what they have achieved so far.

2. They forget that the process to obtain greater dreams is the same they have used to achieve what they have so far. They only need to improve and strengthen the process.

3. Strengthening and improving the process requires changes in thinking and behaviors, and most people are not willing to go through the process of changing themselves. They have become accustomed to their comfort zone.

4. Most people will not make the attempt to change until their backs are against the wall, and most who try will give up if their first few attempts fail.

This is what Dr. Frankl meant by saying that sometimes we must force our minds to the task of looking to the future — the future we desire — our vision.

Finding a reason to look to his future was what George did. I worked with him on the process of clarifying his vision for his relationship with his girlfriend and how to sustain his motivation to make his dream come true — activating the law of attraction. Vision clarification is one of the "how-to" processes at the end of this chapter.

I taught George the vision clarification process, and two weeks later he came back and shared with me how he and his girlfriend, instead of arguing and getting angry at each other, were beginning to talk more about their relationship and getting married, and what type of relationship and family they wanted. They had had a shared vision since they had started dating, but his anger was getting in the way of it and almost doing away with their dreams and desires. Both had something meaningful in mind for their future but they, although most of the work was done by George, had to work at finding their vision.

THE LAW OF ATTRACTION — THOUGHTS AND EMOTIONS ARE CRITICAL

> "You get what you think about — whether you want it or not."
>
> — Esther and Jerry Hicks, *The Law of Attraction*

This is the major premise of the law of attraction and the reason it is always working in our lives. Our personal external world condition reflects the thinking that predominates in our minds. Everything begins in the mind.

What determines how fast the law of attraction works is how prevalent or dominant the thinking is, and how strong your emotions are about what you want or do not want. This thinking accompanied by emotions is called vision. The stronger your vision — how often you think and how strongly you feel about what you think —the quicker it comes into your life. Oh, one other detail: thoughts and emotions create self-motivation . . . You more willingly and automatically move towards that which you want or do not want through the actions you take. Emotions move you to take action to move toward that which you want or do not want, and the law of attraction attracts it toward you. Your thinking, your emotions, and your actions determine how fast you get it. The law of attraction is always at work, but for it to work in your favor, you must decide to make **positive visioning** a habit in your life. Negative visioning also works just as well, but you do not want that, do you?

YOU ACT ACCORDING TO YOUR MOST DOMINANT THOUGHTS AND EMOTIONS

Many proponents of the law of attraction go as far as teaching that as long as you think about what you desire with a high level of positive emotion, the law of attraction is activated and your desires will automatically come into your life. They also lead people to believe that the positive energy this level of thinking creates is what causes your desires to automatically become a reality in your life. I believe this message has led many people to become disillusioned and frustrated with the philosophy.

The law of attraction philosophy is basically equivalent to the faith philosophy of most religious beliefs, but what the proponents of the law of attraction tend to leave out or underemphasize is that action and skill are required to get desires to begin moving toward your life. Whereas thoughts and emotions are most important, action is also required. Most religious philosophies make you aware that action is required in addition to the faith, belief, and emotions you think and feel towards a desire you have. Once you realize this, you can accelerate the speed at which your desire will come to you. You will always act consistently with your predominant way of thinking. Just like negative and pessimistic thinking generates behaviors (actions) that, for the most part, are self-defeating, positive and optimistic thinking generates behaviors and actions that are more productive and effective.

HOW TO ACTIVATE THE LAW OF ATTRACTION TO FAVOR YOU

To turn your desires, dreams, or goals into reality, you must:

1. Clarify which ones you want to bring to reality;

2. Prioritize them in order of importance or value to your life;

3. Dedicate time to envision them becoming true and experiencing the positive emotions during your envisioning process, just like you will feel them when your desires become real;

4. Follow your heart and your emotions when you get indications of what actions you need to take; and

5. Take what I refer to as effortless consistent action.

ATTRACTING WHAT YOU DESIRE

Below are three ways by which you can begin to attract what you desire to your life.

The Clarifying Desires Process

One question I get frequently from clients is "I want many things for my life — how do I make sure which ones I should attract and in what sequence?"

Peter McWilliams coined the following phrase: "You can have anything you want, but you cannot have everything you want … *all at once*." The words in italics are mine. I believe that you can have everything you want, but not all at once. This has been my experience. I have gotten every major desire I wanted in my life up to now, just not all at once. What you need to do is make sure that you really want what you are wanting and assign a priority to the things you want in sequence of importance to you.

Most people, including you, already know what they want and how important it is to get it (it is a priority). However, some people need reassurance. Here is how you can tell what you should attract to your life:

1.   Desires come to your mind in the form of thoughts or ideas, i.e., "Having a larger home would be so much better for all of us," or "It would be nice if I could make more money to be able to buy a better car."

2.   One of these three options crosses your mind: a) You dismiss the thought right away. b) You accept the thought, you contemplate it for a while, and you dismiss it, telling yourself, "It'll never happen because . . ." c) You accept it and contemplate it until a different thought takes you away from it.

3.   This step is the indicator whether you need to pursue your desire or not. If the desire keeps coming to your mind and you know it will improve your life without causing harm to others, then this is your mind, heart, and subconscious mind telling you that it is something you can and should bring into your life. You need to begin planting the thought of it permanently in your mind. This is the first step to activating the law of attraction and the beginning of a new vision for your life.

Authorities on the law of attraction teach that the moment you decide in your mind and heart that you definitely want something to come into your life, what you desire starts moving in your direction immediately, and the resources you need to get it start aligning to help you get it. Most leave one thing out of the equation: the moment you decide with certainty that you want something in your life, your self-motivation starts moving you toward your desire. This mutual attraction accelerates the realization of your desire.

Remember my client George? He found himself on Step 3 when the thought that he needed to do something came to his mind enough times until he decided to do something about it. He wanted to save his relationship. The frequent thought that he might lose his relationship kept coming to his mind. He acted by asking his friends if they knew someone who could help him. Then he came to see me once he got the recommendation. Then he found out that just being able to control his anger was not enough. Now that he is better able to control his anger, he wants to develop his relationship to a higher level. He needs to bring that to his life, and he knows it is a high priority for him.

Too many people act out of emergency or necessity. They wait until they find themselves in some sort of trouble. Then, and only then, they do something about it. However, a great number of people never do anything, although they know they should, because their thought or idea meets the criteria of Step 3 in the desire clarification process. They finally do something mostly when their desire requires significant action steps that disrupt the status quo of their lives. Too many people live unfulfilled lives because in their minds, they think they cannot bring their higher aspirations to reality. Do not let this happen to you. Read Step 3 in the desire clarification process. Decide to pursue your desires and make them reality.

How Do I Know Which Desire to Work On?

The desire clarification process helps you identify which desires you should bring into your life. How do you figure out which desires you should work on?

Let us say that the thought of buying a larger home keeps coming to your mind, but the thought of taking your family on a fun and long vacation abroad also keeps coming to your mind and your family keeps bringing this up as well. Which desire should you attract first, knowing that if you go on vacation, you will spend a considerable amount of money, causing you to postpone the purchase of your larger home, but if you purchase the home you will have to postpone your major family vacation for an undetermined period of time because of all the extra expenses you will incur with the purchase of the home?

The answer is already within you. You only need to listen to the deeper part of your being, which is your subconscious and your emotions. This is the spiritual part of your being. You reach this part, and you learn to listen to it through relaxation and meditation, and it is actually easy. Here is how you do this process, based on your example:

1. Relax. Relaxation releases the stress caused by your indecision.

2. Meditate. Continue breathing deeply and focus your attention on the different options you are trying to select from, one at a time. Let go of any evaluation or judgmental thoughts such as: "Oh, but it's going to be so hard." "Which one is easiest to accomplish?" "This will take a lot longer." In this step, you are simply noticing what your desires are.

3. Notice how you feel when you think about each one, when you spend time imagining each one separately as being part of your life. The one that gives you the better feelings such as satisfaction, peace, happiness, and/or excitement — without judging or evaluating — is the one you should plant in your mind to bring to reality.

   NOTE: In my personal experience and my experience as a life coach, most people already know what they want. Those who need to clarify their desires can decide after doing this three-step meditation. However, if you need further clarification, you can add another step to the previous three.

4. Do not hurry your decision. You are dealing with your future here. If you were not able to decide through the three-step clarification process above, take time to journal about each desire you have. Journaling is a form of meditation if you do it in a quiet place with no interruptions or distractions, and you breathe and relax as you think, write, and feel.

5. Write down what you visualized and what you felt about each one during the first three steps. Write in more detail about how your life and the lives of others will improve by you achieving each desire. Keep the visualizing and writing process going every day as much as possible. You will get the answer you seek.

VISIONING MEDITATION TO ACCELERATE ATTRACTION

This meditation is based on many scientific research experiments done in sports, mind-body medicine and energy healing, and motivation and achievement to demonstrate the power of the mind through imagery and visualization to influence desired results. The undeniable principle, demonstrated by many experiments, is that the brain interprets imaginary information as real because it uses most of the same areas when we imagine something as when we actually see it or experience it in our physical world.

People experience this phenomenon frequently in their lives. For example, many times when you get hungry, you imagine the type of food that you would want to eat, and most of the time you end up consuming that food or a suitable substitute for it. This power of our own mind is what frequently works against us when we imagine and desire something significant in our lives that would be beneficial for ourselves and others. Instead of allowing the thought to settle in our minds, we tell ourselves that it is not possible or it will be too hard to get.

This power of imagination is also a major factor in people developing unhealthy addictions or unhealthy and non-productive behaviors. Such people allow the thought to settle in their minds through repeated imagining and behavior; once it is revealed to be hurting them and others, the thought and the imagination toward it are so strong that they give up trying or find it very difficult to give it up.

A general principle of behavior is that we learn everything through suggestion and most learning happens subconsciously. Suggestion is the repeated thoughts and images we allow within ourselves through our own thinking, and the repeated thoughts and images to which we expose ourselves in our external environment. We learn most things subconsciously because we learn from every suggestion to which we are exposed without realizing that we are learning. The more repeated the exposure to any suggestion, the stronger and more permanent the learning is. This is how each person develops a style of thinking and behavior.

Now that you have a greater understanding of how your brain/mind learns, this understanding empowers you to use your own ability to think about and imagine your own desires and make the process of realizing them much easier. Visioning meditations are very powerful in developing new habits or patterns of thinking and behaviors that are helpful to you moving toward and attracting your desires. Let us do your visioning meditation.

Part 1 — Your Vision Board

1. Find a quiet place where you can be by yourself for twenty to thirty minutes without noise or interruptions. Relax before and during the activity.

2. Get a sheet of blank paper 8.5 x 11 inches or larger. Have some colored pens or markers on hand as well.

3. Using a colored pen you like, write in the center of the paper the desire you want to realize in your life as a title. For example: "Purchase a larger home in a nicer neighborhood."

4. Using a combination of words and pictures, represent the various ways your life will improve once your desire is realized.

Include as many benefits as you can. When you are done, take a few deep breaths and relax. Continue relaxing and ask yourself how you will feel when this desire is a reality in your life and write down your feelings, surrounding your picture with them. This drawing represents your vision of your life with these desires in it.

Keep this picture pinned up in a place where you can see it frequently, or carry it with you in your pocket or purse and look at it a few times throughout the day.

NOTE: Later on, you can make time to make a more elaborate vision board, if you would like to do so. Many people make large vision boards using magazine cutouts and pictures and keep them posted on a wall. Either way works because what makes the process powerful is meditating on your vision using your vision board as a point of concentration.

Let us do part two of the process, which is the process of meditating.

Part 2 — Meditating on Your Vision

For the meditation, allow yourself fifteen to twenty minutes. Make sure you have your vision board visible. Play relaxing music in the background if it helps you relax.

1. Sit down with your back and your head straight and your feet flat on the floor.

2. Start breathing deeply and with every breath you take, tell yourself softly, "With every deep breath I take, I relax deeper and deeper."

3. Remember to breathe deeply as often as possible through your meditation, but in a way that is comfortable to you.

4. As you continue to relax and breathe deeply, look at the picture of your vision for a couple of minutes, and as you look at it, imagine your desire already being part of your life. Allow yourself to feel the feelings you wrote in your picture and close your eyes.

5. Visualize yourself in your picture and imagine yourself already living the experience of your desire realized. Feel the positive feelings you wrote in your picture.

6. Keep your visualization going for the next ten minutes and allow your mind to show you other benefits or feel other positive emotions, and allow yourself to live your reality within your mind and your heart. You can carry on with positive self-talk about your new life as you imagine yourself living it.

7. After you have visualized for at least ten minutes, slowly open your eyes. Take a few deep breaths and end the meditation. Stand up and stretch for a few minutes.

NOT BEING ABLE TO IMPROVE OUR LIVES IS NOT ANYONE'S FAULT BUT OUR OWN

In this chapter, you have become more aware of the process and the power of vision.

Vision is a natural ability that everyone has. This is how we obtain everything we have obtained so far. Most people are unaware that this is how our brain works. Our lives are the result of our thinking. Everything that is in our lives has germinated in our thinking. Our thoughts create images and sensations that are expressed through emotions and, motivated by these images and sensations, we bring ourselves to where we are.

The purpose of this chapter and lifestyle shift in my Life Transformation Paradigm is to empower ourselves to direct our thoughts and emotions in the direction of our higher aspirations.

Dr. Daniel J. Siegel, in his book *Mindsight: The New Science of Personal Transformation*, describes the mind as "the embodied and relational process that regulates the flow of energy and information within and among us." He further describes the brain as the biological component in the human being through which this energy and information is managed and controlled.

Meditation is one of the most effective methods of managing and controlling our own energy and information created by our own thinking. Practicing visioning meditations enhances and magnifies the power of our positive thoughts, thus causing us to attract and move toward our highest desires. Meditation empowers us to live the life each of us has been designed to live.

In the next chapter, you will learn about how awareness, the fourth lifestyle shift, also empowers us to live a more fulfilling life.

VISION

Are you feeling bored? Are you feeling unchallenged?
Is life a grind and routine, and not utilizing your talent?
Do you do what you do because you have to?
Is life a drag though that is not what you intend to?

Have you lost the vision that once got you excited?
When you lose your vision to burnout, you have decided.
For it is your vision that gets your engine ignited.
Burnout or energy — it is up to us, only we can decide it.

Vision is the vivid picture of a worthy ideal realized.
Vision is the clear picture of your dream that gets you energized.
Vision is the foreseen impact of your ideal on your fellow man.
Vision induces commitment to accomplish it and do all you can.
Vision shows possibilities. With vision, no dream is an impossibility.

In everything you do, you must create an intense vision —
a vision so powerful, clear, and uncluttered,
a vision driven by higher values, desires, and reasons.
Even in routine, you'll be driven by your meaningful vision.

— Dr. Jose M. Baltazar

Lifestyle Shift #4: Awareness—All Learning Happens Through Suggestion, and Most Learning Is Subconscious

"Heading into the 21st century you are no longer a mind and a body; you are a mind-body."

— Sheila Ostrander and Lynn Schroeder,
Super-Learning, 1982

EVERYBODY IS A LEARNER

I have been a counselor and instructor for almost fifty years. One area I have studied is the process of learning, but I have studied it out of the traditional model of teaching and learning that most government-funded institutions practice.

When I graduated from the community college I attended, I started working for it in the information processing department. Within a short time of working in this community college, I found out a fact that immediately caused me to ask the question: if this problem has existed for such a long time, why do educators keep doing the same thing over and over? The surprising thing is that even at present, the same problem exists within public education, and when you put together public education with private education, the problem still is a major one. I researched this information through various educational journals and websites, and I found out that only about 25–30 percent of all students who enter college graduate.

You can see why I decided to look somewhere else to help my students improve their performance as learners after I got established in the community college system. In the early '80s, I became familiar with a totally different system of teaching and learning called accelerated learning, which was developed in Europe by a genius whose name was Dr. Georgi Lozanov.

Dr. Lozanov's method of teaching and learning looks at students as life learners, not as school learners, and consequently his approach seeks to develop the whole person instead of just focusing on the subject being taught. As a teacher is teaching a specific subject, lessons are delivered in such a way that other aspects of living are being learned.

Students are also learning in areas such as improving their self-esteem, developing self-motivation, and developing a love for lifelong learning, self-sufficiency, resilience, and interpersonal relationships, to name a few. Since all aspects of personal development and self-leadership are included in the lessons along with the subject being taught, this form of learning is referred as "Suggestopedia" or suggestive teaching and learning. It is satisfying and fulfilling for the teacher to see how students transform themselves after being exposed to this type of learning experience.

Along with my full-time position at the college, I was teaching an intro-ductory course in data processing to adult limited English speakers with no more than a fourth-grade education. I started using accelerated learning strategies to teach them about computers, and I was surprised at the positive results I saw in my students. They could learn the material and continue taking classes with the goal of graduating with a vocational technical education degree. Along with teaching information processing principles, I was teaching study skills, self-esteem, and self-motivation.

Most of these students would not have even considered starting college, and yet they did and moved on to their degree programs.

Motivated by my own observations, I decided in 1988 to change careers to become a full-time counselor and instructor within the community college system. In 1988, working for El Paso Community College in El Paso, Texas, I immersed myself in learning more about accelerated learning. The practice of accelerated learning would significantly change my life and that of hundreds of students I had the opportunity to teach and counsel, and later clients I have coached as a health, wellness, and lifestyle coach.

HOW WE BECOME WHO WE ARE

Most people learn about awareness through meditation. Interestingly, I learned about awareness through accelerated learning. One of the foundational principles of it is that we learn everything we know through suggestion, and most of what we learn in life is through subconscious suggestion. We start learning even before we are born.

A baby in the womb can feel the emotions of her mother. Those emotions will affect the personality of the baby. This is a perfect example of subconscious learning. The baby learns without knowing that she is learning. Another perfect example is how we become who we are. We mostly become the type of person we are subconsciously. We have learned most of our behaviors subconsciously. We did not go to "How-to-Be-You University" to learn to be who we are. Only afterwards, when we think back with awareness, can we tell at times how we learned to think and behave a certain way.

I will share a personal example of subconscious learning with you. I have always been a money saver. This behavior has been beneficial for me throughout my life. However, on some occasions, it can be a setback. Such was the case with starting my own business after retirement. Due to my saving habits, I became cautious about how I spent and invested my money. Although I have done well financially, this carefulness held me back from making riskier investments I needed to make to get my business to a higher level.

Now that I must make investments that are riskier than I am used to making, I realize I learned such carefulness from my dad. I always gave credit to my dad for my saving habits, but recently I realized I am fearful of losing money as I consider making larger investments to grow my business. To overcome this fear, I am learning to be an entrepreneur through training and association with other entrepreneurs and businesspeople.

HOW WE LEARN SUBCONSCIOUSLY

We learn subconsciously in three ways — exposure, repetition, and association. Most of the time we are not aware that we are learning. Like most everything else, subconscious learning can be good and it can be bad.

Exposure: We naturally expose ourselves to environments that are pleasing to our senses. Unless we question these environments — and most of the time we do not — we unconditionally accept the teachings of such environments. The more we expose ourselves to these environments, the more we learn from them without realizing it. We are learning all the time, but most learning happens without us processing it consciously.

Repetition: Frequent exposure to the same types of environments exposes us to main themes and language frequently repeated. These words, phrases, and themes eventually become engrained in our memory and without realizing it, we accept them as normal and they eventually become part of our behavior. Another effect is that even though initially we do not like certain repeated messages, we continue listening to them until eventually the objections disappear and we become oblivious to them. Our minds end up accepting them. This is subconscious learning.

Association: Learning by association occurs when we start hanging around frequently and/or spending long periods of time with other individuals. We do this naturally and intentionally when we get along with others, and we like them because they have things and values in common with us.

The human brain is like a sponge. It takes in data quickly and quickly turns that data into information to learn from it. Anything that is pleasing to our senses and arouses pleasing sensations and emotions becomes quick and easy learning for our brain. The other great ability of the brain is its amazing capacity to adapt. Sometimes we may not like someone or something initially, but if we keep hanging around, we eventually end up liking it in most cases. Have you ever listened to a song for the first time and not liked it, but as the media keeps playing it and you keep hearing it, you eventually like it or accept it? This is subconscious learning.

AWARENESS IS THE ANSWER FOR HIGHER QUALITY OF LEARNING

As we grow and live life, we always are learning. Awareness is the skill that helps us tell whether the learning will help us or work against us. Remember, we learn most things subconsciously, which means we do not evaluate them — we simply take the information through our mind, body, senses, and emotions. This is the reason most people will ask at one time or another, "Why am I this way? Why do I keep doing this? Why am I not able to change?" These are questions that imply that we want to improve but do not seem to be able to overcome personal obstacles.

Developing higher levels of awareness helps us understand why we behave the way we do. Awareness helps us understand prior experiences and how they have affected our lives and empowers us to change. With greater awareness, we learn to evaluate the learning we are exposed to and accept good learning and screen out bad learning. Awareness increases our emotional intelligence, develops our problem-solving abilities, and helps us make better choices in life.

MEDITATION IS THE VEHICLE TO GREATER AWARENESS

Dr. Jon Kabat-Zinn popularized mindfulness and mindfulness meditation in the United States. In his book *Mindfulness for Beginners*, he discusses awareness and defines it as the ability to gently focus, pay attention, and experience the sensations created by what you focus on. From page 45 of his book, I quote:

> "But it is essential that you know right from the beginning that it is not the breath sensations, or sounds, or even our thoughts when we are paying attention to thoughts that are most important. What is most important but most easily missed, taken for granted, and not experienced is the awareness that feels and knows directly, without thinking, that breathing is going on in this moment, that hearing is going on in this moment, that thoughts are moving through the sky-like space of the mind at this moment. As we have seen, it is the awareness that is of primary importance, no matter what the objects are that we are paying attention to."

According to Dr. Kabat-Zinn, awareness is something we naturally possess. We are it (awareness) already because it is naturally part of us. He states on page 46:

> "And that awareness is already ours. It is already available, already complete, already capable of holding and knowing (non-concep-tually) anything and everything in our experience inwardly and outwardly, no matter how big, how trivial, or how momentous. That is simply the property of awareness. And you already have it! Or perhaps it would be more accurate to say, you already are it."

Most people, although they have been given the property of awareness, have their awareness dormant or inactive. They have allowed this to happen because they have become so immersed in the superficial existence that money, places, entertainment, technology, media, and a stressful life offer.

These things are not bad in and of themselves, but through subconscious learning of what society offers, people become unaware individuals more susceptible to manipulation, misinformation, and misguidance. Lack of awareness affects most people, regardless of economic or societal status.

GREATER AWARENESS THROUGH MEDITATION OFFERS MANY BENEFITS

Earlier in Chapter 2, I mentioned some of the health and wellness benefits that the practice of relaxation and meditation offers. Before I discuss the benefits of gaining greater awareness through meditation, allow me to list again what a consistent practice of relaxation and meditation can do:

- Increase energy and stamina;
- Increase longevity and promote healthier aging;
- Promote healthy sleep;
- Reduce oxidative stress;
- Oxygenate the brain and the blood stream;
- Contribute to the health and growth of neurons in the brain;
- Contribute to the decalcification of vessels;
- Improve blood circulation and pressure;
- Help improve body balance, coordination, and grounding;
- Contribute to the repair of cells at the molecular level;
- Increase mental, physical, and spiritual (emotional) health;
- Promotes states of calmness, peace, and satisfaction with life; and
- Evokes the body/mind/spirit healing and wellness response.

In addition to what relaxation and meditation can do for you, here is a list of how your behavior can be positively influenced by the practice:

- Your powers of intuition increase. You make much better distinctions about the information and the intention of messages (suggestion) you receive from the environment.

- You become more relaxed under pressure and are capable of handling stressful events without suffering the damaging effects of heavy stress.

- Your naturally become a better problem solver.

- You know with certainty your purpose and mission in life.

- You become more hopeful and optimistic.

- You become more self-motivated and self-reliant.

- You become more resilient.

- You become more connected to everything and everyone else.

- You become emotionally balanced and remain calm, cool, and collected when you live through emotionally charged events.

- You grow in your spirituality.

Although these benefits will not be realized all at once, you will start experiencing some of them sooner than others depending on your own personal needs.

Do you see now why relaxation and meditation is at the core of my Life Transformation Paradigm model? Living a healthy, happy, long, peaceful, and prosperous life without stress is possible. Regardless of what your religious or spiritual value system is, you can integrate relaxation and meditation into it and even make it a much stronger and beneficial spiritual experience.

Yes! You can live a happy, healthy, long, and prosperous life in a continuous state of peace and without suffering the ravages of a stressful life.

AWARENESS DEVELOPMENT
EXERCISES AND MEDITATIONS

Developing greater awareness does not happen from one day to the next. It is a lifelong process. However, you start noticing differences soon after starting the process. Meditation is the best way to develop awareness, but you can use other methods along with your meditation practice to speed up the process. In this section, I will share with you two meditations and two alternative methods to start your growth in this area.

MEDITATION TO DEVELOP GREATER
ATTENTION AND CONCENTRATION

Attention and concentration are qualities of awareness. Greater attention and concentration improve the ability to obtain information, process it, make sense of it, and distinguish how helpful it is in making better choices. This exercise can become part of your daily meditation practice.

1. Sit comfortably in a quiet place where you will not be disturbed for twenty minutes.

2. Begin by relaxing for about five minutes, taking deep, relaxing breaths and keeping your attention on your breath. If any thoughts come to your mind, gently let them go and bring your attention back to your breath. You can close your eyes if you find it helpful to concentrate.

3. Open your eyes and continue relaxing by taking slow, deep breaths. Look at the wall in front of you and find something to fix your vision on. It can be anything, like a picture, a power outlet, a nail, a pin, or even a blank spot. Once you decide what to fix your eyes on, keep your attention on it for a period of ten minutes. As you keep looking at the object, gently let go of any thoughts that come to your mind. Feel free to blink when you need to. If too many thoughts come to your mind, then you can feel free to think

—but only about the object or spot you are looking at. Doing this will help you keep your focus and attention only on that.

4. Once the ten minutes pass, close your eyes again and relax for five minutes, keeping your attention on your deep relaxing breathing and gently letting go of any thoughts that come to your mind.

5. At the end of the five minutes, open your eyes and take a few deep breaths and end the meditation.

MEDITATION TO BECOME MORE AWARE OF YOUR BODY

Greater awareness of your body helps you be more sensitive to the physical states of it. You learn to sense and recognize the different physical sensations you experience throughout the day. This physical awareness helps you respond to yourself in a more caring and accepting manner and leads you to develop healthier ways to treat yourself physically.

1. Follow the directions below as you continue to remain relaxed and at peace. The instructions guide you through a scan of your entire body, one section at a time. As each section is mentioned, place your attention on that section of your body and its parts and allow yourself to notice any sensations. If you notice sensations of discomfort, allow these parts of your body to relax and imagine letting go of the discomfort with every relaxing breath you take. If you feel sensations of relaxation, health, and wellness, enjoy the feelings and sensations of good health with every relaxing breath you take. Remember, if other thoughts come to your mind, gently let them go.

2. Focus your attention on your entire head and face down, to your neck. Take a deep breath and let your head, face, and neck relax deeply. Continue breathing deeply, and relax more and more.

3. Now, notice your throat, shoulders, arms, and hands down to your fingertips. Take a deep, relaxing breath and allow your throat, shoulders, arms, and hands down to your fingertips to relax deeply. Continue breathing deeply and relax more and more.

4. Now, notice your chest, your heart, your lungs, and your upper back. Take a deep, relaxing breath and allow your chest, heart, lungs, and your upper back to relax more and more. Continue breathing deeply and relax more and more.

5. Now, focus your attention on your stomach and midsection, including the middle of your back. Take a deep relaxing breath and allow your stomach, entire midsection, and the middle of your back to relax deeply. Continue breathing deeply and relax more and more.

6. Now focus your attention on the lower part of your body, from your lower abdomen and lower back down. Notice the lower part of your body down to the tip of your spinal cord, your colon, your sexual organs, your legs, and your feet down to your toes, including the soles of your feet. Continue breathing deeply and allow yourself to relax more and more, deeper and deeper.

7. Remain silent for about five minutes and continue relaxing, and allow yourself to feel how relaxed your entire body is. This is the feeling of peace, health, and wellness.

8. Keep the feelings of health, wellness, peace, and relaxation in your mind, body, and spirit. Bring your attention back to the room. Feel the chair you are sitting on and notice the room's environment: how cold or warm it is, the smells in the air, and any noises. Become more and more aware of the room, slowly open your eyes, and take a long, deep, energizing breath. Stand up and stretch your arms and your entire body and come back to your seat.

MEDITATION TO DEVELOP SENSORY AWARENESS

A typical way to start growing in awareness is to develop greater acuity of your senses. The process is rather easy. You only need to practice this technique as often as possible. Sensory acuity can be developed through intentional mindful observation or through meditation.

As you continue to practice and exercise your senses, you will notice that you become more consciously aware of your environment. As you become more consciously aware of what goes on in your environment, you become less distracted and more capable of distinguishing what is helpful or harmful to you. Your mind becomes sharper and more observant, and capable of taking greater amounts of information and sorting through it to make better decisions. Let us practice.

INTENTIONAL MINDFUL OBSERVATION

The following are examples of intentional mindful observation:

1. Anywhere you are at any time during the day, take five minutes and notice what sounds or noises you can perceive as you pay attention in silence. At other times, you can take five minutes and lightly touch something close to you, anything, and feel it with your hand. You get the idea. Practice two or three times a day using a different sense each time. Make sure you use your five senses alternatively.

2. Once a day, for ten to twenty minutes, stop what you are doing and use your five senses to feel different things in your environment through your touch, hearing, smell, taste, or vision, and notice the sensations and/or feelings that arise within you as you sense what is in your immediate environment with each and all of your senses.

SENSORY AWARENESS MEDITATION

Through meditation, you can develop greater awareness much faster and make sensory awareness meditations part of your daily relaxation and meditation practice. In this exercise, you basically do similar activities to mindful observations. The difference is that you perform these activities in your imagination. Doing these imagery or visualization meditations expands your powers of creativity in addition to your powers of awareness because you are creating the images in your mind instead of using your physical senses. You are going to love doing these meditations.

Because we live life with all our senses and emotions, performing this exercise in a different imaginary place each time you do it trains you to be more aware of your environment wherever you are, and trains your mind to make finer distinctions and observations about everything going on around you. This translates to practical abilities like greater alertness, faster and more accurate interpretations of information, and a greater ability to make better choices when being presented with or considering different alternatives.

Let us do the meditation below:

1. Sit comfortably in a quiet place where you will not be disturbed for twenty minutes.

2. Take five minutes to relax. Close your eyes and begin relaxing by taking deep, relaxing breaths and keeping your attention on your breathing. If any thoughts come to your mind, gently let them go and bring your attention back to your breath.

3. With your eyes closed and taking relaxing breaths, imagine yourself in a place where you have been before where you experienced rest, peace, and relaxation. This place could be a park, forest, beach, mountain, or any other place where you experienced peace, rest, happiness, and/or relaxation. If you cannot think of a place like this, allow yourself to imagine and create a place where you

know you would be able to feel peace, rest, and relaxation. Take your time to create and experience your place of peace and rest.

4. As you see yourself in your peaceful place, you will notice how you can experience it using all your senses and your emotions. What are you doing in this place? Are you sitting, standing, walking? Notice what you are doing. How do you feel being there? Are there any objects you can touch or feel with your body, your hands, or perhaps with your feet, or any other part of your body? How do these objects feel to you as you touch them? Notice everything in this place. What do you see? Describe some of the things you see to yourself. Do any of the things you see have a smell or aroma to them? Describe the aromas you perceive. Are there any noises or sounds that you can hear in your place of rest? Describe what you hear and how you feel when you hear any of the sounds with more attention. Are there any items you can drink or eat and taste and enjoy? Perhaps some delicious food, fruits, snacks, and/or drinks?

5. Take time to be in your place of peace and rest and experience it with all your senses. This exercise takes about twenty minutes to do.

Awareness is a natural state of being, but it is dormant in many people. Meditation and attention are the vehicles to awakening it and expanding it within ourselves.

WISDOM

Wisdom is the most important value.
Few people have it as a goal
because it's not easy to practice,
nor can you give it material worth.
Wisdom does not come automatically.
Wisdom must be sought.
Wisdom comes from within.
In the classroom, it cannot be taught.

Wisdom is an attitude you develop by
looking beyond the material and looking at
what happens to you in a positive light and criteria.
You grow in wisdom when you seek to learn
from every experience in life.
Look for the lessons in every experience,
whether it is good or bad.
To learn and improve from all of them:
this is what it is to be wise.

You do not become wise overnight.
It is a process of growth.
You become wise when you learn to smile at life,
even when it gives you a low blow.
You develop wisdom when you look for the good
in every adversity of life.
To be happy with what you have left,
but always continue to try.

You are wise when your actions are
driven by spiritual values.
The material will end.
Spiritual values will help you move forward
even when you think you can't.
You've become wise when you learn to see good in others
even when you do not like their ways.
Seek first to understand others,
then to be understood,
and your relationships will be better in every way.

Wisdom is to learn to recognize
what builds you up
and what causes you harm.
To know that even though something
makes you feel good,
it will harm you over the long run.
Wisdom is being open-minded and
wanting to learn and to grow.
It's to share your knowledge with others,
not to keep it or withdraw.

The final test of wisdom will come at the end of the road.
When you peacefully get off the train of life and
can be thankful for the trip to your Lord.
Seek to become wise for it is a most important value.
Few people have wisdom as a goal
because it's not easy to practice,
nor can you attach to it any material worth.

— Dr. Jose M. Baltazar

CHAPTER 7

Lifestyle Shift #5: Living Is Holistic and Systemic— Mind, Body, and Spirit

"It is interesting that the words 'whole' and 'health' come from the same root (the Old English *hal*, as in 'hale and hearty'). So, it should come as no surprise that the unhealthiness of our world today is in direct proportion to our inability to see it as a whole. Systems Thinking is a discipline for seeing wholes."

— Peter M. Senge, PhD,
The Fifth Discipline

YOU ARE A SYSTEM AND LIVE WITHIN A SYSTEM

One of my early career experiences was working in the computer field. It was back in the early '70s up to the mid-'80s. Back then, businesses required computers consisting of many pieces of equipment to be able to automate their operations. I used to write software and operate the equipment. What this experience taught me and engrained in my mind forever was the concept and importance of how everything works as a system, including living life.

Even today, think about a computer or cell phone and consider what happens when one thing goes wrong with it. The whole apparatus stops working. For example, let us say that the screen of the phone or computer stops working — will you be able to use it? The idea of a system is that if anything goes wrong in one part of the system, the whole system suffers. It does not work the same; its performance is affected negatively. Everything works like this in life. Everything and everyone is a system, and everything and everyone functions or lives as a part of a larger system.

By definition, a system is a set of components brought together to accomplish a task or a set of tasks. And by definition, anything that helps a system perform its task(s) better also contributes to a larger system performing its tasks better, and so on and so on. The opposite is also true. Anything that goes wrong in a system reduces its level of performance, and the reduction of that system's performance also reduces the performance of the larger system(s).

LIVING IS HOLISTIC AND SYSTEMIC

Living our lives is also holistic and systemic. Holism is the awareness and understanding that everything and everyone exists as a part of a whole. Systems thinking is the practice of holism. Systems thinking is concerned with the effects that our actions and those of others have on the systems in which we live. Awareness tells us that in order for the systems in which we live to work at their best, we must take care of ourselves the very best we can in order for these systems to be able to also work at their best. Holistic living and systems thinking start with each individual.

You perhaps live in a family system and work within a system that employs you. You also participate in a church system, city system, county system, state system, country system, world system, and so on. If you apply systems and holistic thinking, you start seeing the importance you play in all these systems. Anything good or bad happening in your system has a ripple effect throughout all the systems you live in.

IT ALL STARTS AND ENDS WITH YOU

Bringing it down to you, then: you are a system yourself and by definition, as a system, you are a set of components brought together to accomplish certain tasks. Thus, the title of this book: *Live A Healthy, Happy, Long Life and Prosper Without Stress.* You are here on Earth for a reason and you are on Earth to live the best life possible because living it benefits you and all the other systems to which you belong. The other part you need to be aware of is the components that make up who you are. Depending on your personal beliefs, you have two or three main components: your mind, your body . . . and your spirit if you believe in some form of spiritual philosophy.

Most people want their life to be better in some way, but they are not aware of the systems and holistic principles. They try to improve their life by changing only one, or at the most two, of the three components that make up who they are.

As an example, I worked a short while ago with a young man who suffered from anxiety due to his insecurity about his life in the future, and the fear of catching the coronavirus because he was being required to work by his employer. He asked me to help him with his anxiety.

In his mind, he had a mental illness problem. He thought that by me teaching him relaxation and meditation techniques, he could solve his anxiety issue. Of course, I know that would be helpful to him; however, to be able to resolve the problem much more effectively and thoroughly, I explained to him that I would have to also inquire about and help him with his physical and spiritual components. He agreed.

If one of your components is not working well, the functioning of the other components is also affected adversely, and if you only fix the component that is causing your problem, it does not mean that your other components will automatically be restored to the way they were functioning before the problem appeared. You must also tend to the other components.

As I continued working with this young man, we looked into his physical body and also his spiritual state, and in addition to teaching him mind techniques for his anxiety, I recommended a physical exercise and nutrition program for his brain functioning and overall health. He also shared with me that his spiritual beliefs were Christian and that he had stopped his Christian practices, but that he believed in God and wanted to get back to practicing his prayers with strong faith. I recommended that he practice his prayers in a state of relaxation and to play slow instrumental music as he was praying to help him remain relaxed and at peace. I also taught him some relaxed visualizations to be able to feel God closer to him. He took on this holistic approach to resolving his anxiety issue and to date, he has kept his anxiety in check.

What is the area in your life that you want to improve? Your physical health, your mental health, your spiritual health, your marriage, your relationship with your children or other members of your family, your finances, your career, your mission in life? Are you going through some form of adversity? Whatever it is, you must approach the solution in a systemic and holistic way.

YOUR MIND

Your mind is your most powerful resource because without the ability to think, your body becomes a vegetable and it dies rather quickly. And yet, your mind resides in your brain and your brain is part of your body. In addition, you experience the spiritual through your mind and your brain.

This is a perfect example of the systemic and holistic nature of your existence. If your brain (the body) does not function correctly, you cannot think effective thoughts (the mind), and if neither of them function effectively, you cannot experience the spiritual effectively — and by the same token, if you are not living according to your spiritual beliefs, most likely your mind and body are also out of sync.

START BY CHANGING YOUR MINDSET

Your mind is the totality of your thoughts. Your way or style of thinking and your emotional states determine the level of the health of your mind. Your thoughts and your emotions determine how you act and feel about the condition of your life.

No one is perfect, but everyone desires something better in life. We are designed to always aspire to something better. People who say they are perfectly happy with their life the way it is are lying to themselves. What they have done is quieted their inner spiritual voice and given up out of self-doubt and/or fear. Most of these individuals have replaced their higher aspirations for small desires of the moment, such as buying a new dress, a better meal, a better television set, a vacation, etc., and settled into a daily routine while their dreams get out of reach.

How you think and how you act is called your mindset. As the word implies, your mind is set to think and behave in a certain way. What should determine whether you need to change your mindset or not is if you have thought about pursuing a higher worthwhile desire and if you are not working on it; if so, then you know you must change your mindset. Your present mindset has you stuck.

In Chapter 3, I shared with you the process to clarify your desires and be able to tell if you should pursue them or not. Once you determine that you want to pursue a desire, you need to start by changing your mindset. The process of changing your mindset is an on-going process. You know your mindset is changing when you decide to start taking steps of action to achieve your desire. The steps you take do not have to be gigantic steps. What matters is that you consistently move toward your dream, goal, or desire.

CHANGE YOUR LIMITING BELIEFS

Your beliefs act as filters in living your life. Every decision you make and every action you take go through your belief system to make a choice or determine whether or not to go ahead and perform the necessary action(s) once the choice is made. Everything you do is checked against your belief system, without exception.

Daily life routines do not appear to be this way, but they are. When you make choices and take actions habitually, the process of filtering happens without you realizing it because making the choice and performing the checking against your beliefs have become habits or automatic processes of your mind. More frequently than not, it is habitual behaviors that prevent us from improving our lives. We become comfortable with the routines of a lifestyle that is not promoting our growth anymore. When we think about achieving a greater desire but focus on the obstacles and challenges of getting it, we may end up giving it up. Our belief system keeps us stuck in our comfort zone.

Beliefs that keep you in your comfort zone are mostly good beliefs, but they limit you from attaining greater desires you know you should obtain. These are the beliefs that make you think thoughts like "I make a good living, I should be satisfied," "I love my children, I must take care of them myself," "Why keep busting my behind, I'm doing OK," and so on. There are some beliefs that stop you from even considering the possibilities. These are the beliefs that make you think thoughts like "I can't," "It's impossible for me," "I've always failed before," "It's not for me," and so on.

STRENGTHEN YOUR POSITIVE BELIEFS

You also have many positive beliefs already. These beliefs have brought you to your life the way it is at present. Positive beliefs are those that move you to bring additional good things and achievements to your life. These beliefs cause you to act when you want something in your life which is of benefit to you, your loved ones, and/or your community and which you feel certain you can get or achieve. For example, let us say you get the thought of buying something for a friend. You know he has been wanting to get it but has not been able to afford it. You make the necessary considerations, you decide you *can* afford it, and you buy it for him. Your beliefs of friendship and affordability gave you the certainty to go ahead and buy it.

However, if the desire to be obtained is significantly more ambitious and further into the future, most people will give up the desire even though deep within, they know they would like to obtain it. Larger desires, dreams, and goals cause most people to doubt their ability and capacity to reach them. Instead of giving up your desires, you need to strengthen your good beliefs so that you can develop your level of certainty that you can achieve them.

By changing negative beliefs to positive ones and strengthening your good beliefs, you increase your level of ability and certainty to obtain any higher desire that comes to you. At the end of this chapter, I will share with you mind-body techniques that help you accomplish this — but first, let us discuss the care of your physical body.

YOUR BODY

Your body is a complex system. But like any other system, there are some basic needs it has in order to remain healthy and in balance. Your body needs to be properly fed, and it must also be kept in good physical condition through consistent exercise. There is plenty of information available on different kinds of exercise you can do, and there is also plenty of information about different nutritional plans and diets to follow.

When I work with clients, I find that most are well-informed about the need to eat healthier and exercise. In addition, because information in these areas is readily available, most of them are familiar with the kinds of food they should be eating and different types of exercise. In these areas, information is not the problem. The problem is in developing the habits of eating healthy food and exercising. Most people are not sticking to a consistent practice.

In this section, I discuss the basics of nutrition and exercise; however, my main intention is to teach you mind conditioning techniques that will help you naturally develop the permanent habits of eating healthier and exercising. In my experiential observations, lack of knowledge about the importance of practicing healthy nutrition and exercise is not the problem. The problem is developing the permanent habit, and this is what I would like to address and teach you in this part of my book.

THE BASICS OF NUTRITION

Nutrition is important in the management of stress and in the prevention and treatment of disease. Oxidative stress is an imbalance between free radical production and the antioxidant defenses in our bodies and is a major cause of disease development. Oxidative stress is aggravated by a stressful lifestyle, unhealthy nutrition, and lack of exercise. Proper nutrition is important in the prevention and management of chronic disease. A balanced, nutritious diet is an important component of the mind-body-spirit system.

In addition to the basics of nutrition, in this section you will learn the skill of mindful eating. Mindful eating teaches you to appreciate food and to exercise control in eating proper portions and developing healthier eating habits. You also learn how mindful eating can be used for managing weight and improving mental health.

Mindful eating means that you focus on your food and the act of eating when you eat. By focusing your mind on the act of eating, you become more aware of the kinds of food you bring into your body and the effect this food has on your body and your mental and physical health. You also chew your food more thoroughly; thus, you become full and satisfied with less food. You become aware of enjoying and savoring the food you eat, and you appreciate the fact that you have food to nurture yourself more.

Eating becomes an experience and not just an activity. The last exercise in this lesson walks you through the experience of eating mindfully.

It is interesting to note that even though people are more aware of the importance of eating a healthier diet to remain healthy and for disease or weight management, most are not aware of the importance of eating healthier for stress management. This segment on nutrition and mindful eating, and movement and exercise, can help raise your awareness in this regard.

NUTRITION AFFECTS YOUR EMOTIONS

Emotions are intrinsically connected with stress, illness, and chronic disease. From your own experience, you know that when you experience sadness, anger, frustration, impatience, and so on, you feel it somewhere in your body, and this feeling does not make your body feel good. For example, Dr. David Perlmutter, in his book *Grain Brain*, states that *"a diet heavy in inflammatory carbs and low in healthy fats messes with the mind in more ways than one – affecting risk not just for dementia but for common neurological ailments such as ADHD, anxiety disorder, Tourette's syndrome, mental illness, migraines, and even autism."*

Repressed anger or resentment, uncontrolled stress, anxiety, and fear can have devastating effects on the mind, body, and spirit. Unresolved negative emotions trigger the flight-or-fight response, which in turn sets off a chain of physiological events in which blood pressure rises and muscles contract. When this happens frequently or for extended periods of time, symptoms such as headaches, muscle pain, cramps, or insomnia start manifesting in the body, and eventually chronic conditions may develop such as heart disease, colitis, autoimmune disorders, and gastrointestinal disorders.

Negative emotions can be regulated through proper nutrition, physical exercise, and mind techniques. Most people forget the mind-body-spirit connection and when negative emotional states such as angry behavior become acute, they attempt to regulate their emotions mostly though medication.

Dr. Ruth Leyse-Wallace, in her book *Linking Nutrition to Mental Health: A Scientific Exploration*, reminds us of the importance of managing emotions through better nutrition. She documents how a lack of proper nutrition also plays a critical role in mental illnesses or conditions such as depression, anxiety, hyperactivity, and attention deficit disorder; she also documents how these and other challenges contribute significantly to physical diseases such as obesity, high cholesterol, and eating disorders.

Most people know but ignore the fact that a healthier diet is also helpful to the brain and, therefore, helpful in regulating emotional health. When people think about dieting or eating better, they usually think of preventing physical illness or preventing an illness from getting worse, keeping a nicer shape, losing weight, or living longer, but rarely consider that it will improve their emotional health.

You must also relate eating healthier to better emotional health. Emotional states or emotional moods are a function of the brain. If you eat better, your brain functions much better. If your brain functions better, you will also experience improvement in your emotions. When you eat healthier foods you feel better, you experience healthier emotions, you learn much better, and you experience better health, live longer, have a better-looking body, and prevent mental and physical diseases.

HEALTHY NUTRITION

Water is essential — our brains are over 80 percent water, and our bodies are 60 percent water by weight. Thus it makes sense that we need to drink plenty of water every day. If you squeeze out the water from the brain, it will shrink like a raisin. One thing that keeps the brain full and vibrant is giving it the amount of water it needs; otherwise, the brain cannot perform the functions it needs to perform in order to maintain good health, good processing of information, and good memory. The same principle applies to the body. Water provides energy to the brain and the body, and energy translates into improved health and learning functions. Unfortunately, most people do not drink the appropriate amount of water needed on a daily basis.

Dr. Fereydoon Batmanghelidj, author of *Water for Health, for Healing, for Life: You're Not Sick, You're Thirsty!*, recommends that every adult person should take at least eight 8-ounce glasses of water every day, distributed throughout the day, not all at once. That's 64 ounces of water per day. Providing your brain and your body with the amount of water it needs will help you improve your mental, emotional, and physical health. He also discusses how chronic dehydration is a major contributor to many known diseases such as hypertension, obesity, high cholesterol and plaque buildup, osteoporosis, repeated strokes, diabetes, Alzheimer's disease, skin problems, and many others.

FOOD IS MEDICINE

Just like the case with water, most people do not eat a healthier and balanced diet. By simply adding healthier foods to your daily eating routine, you will experience noticeable results in your ability to stay alert, focused, and energized. You do not have to entirely give up foods that you enjoy, and at the same time you do not have to make eating better so complicated. I think this is one of the reasons why people do not watch what they eat. Most experts make it so difficult to understand and implement better eating habits.

I like Dr. Barry Sears, author of the book *Enter the Zone*. He draws a very simple chart of a balanced diet and recommends that you imagine that this chart is a plate of food. Whenever you eat a meal, these are the percentages of each category of foods that your meal should have. You also imagine your day and what you eat through the day as one single plate and you do a mental account of each category of foods to check if you have stayed within the recommended percentages. You do this so that if you cannot balance each individual meal, you should at least balance the percentages through the day.

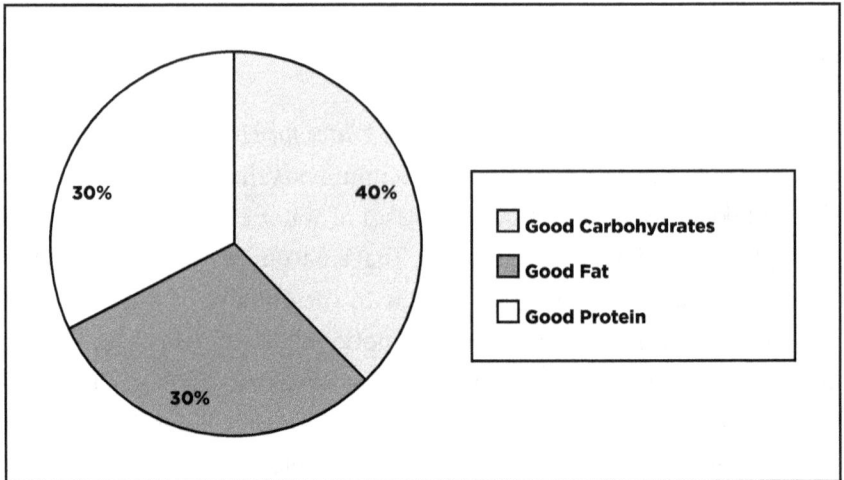

Common sense tells us what we should eat in order to stay healthier and help our body and brain/mind work much better. Dr. Sears' recommendations help you balance your meals throughout the day. You only need to know some basics as to what foods provide good protein, good carbohydrates, and good fat.

Good carbohydrates — For good carbohydrates, you need to eat more vegetables, grains and nuts, and whole grain breads. Eat a variety of them. Eliminate processed white flour products like cookies, doughnuts, sweet breads, cake, pizza, tortillas, and white flour breads. Also eliminate or minimize starchy foods like spaghetti, potato chips, and cereals. Eliminate products that contain white sugar and artificial sweeteners.

Good protein — To get good protein, you can eat beef. Eat beef that does not have too much fat or grease and that is labeled "grass-fed" or "organic" or "free-range." These labels mean the animals have not been raised with chemicals or hormones. You can also eat poultry without the skin and that is also labeled as indicated for beef. Fish and other seafood options are great sources of protein and are recommended over beef and poultry. Just make sure you eat fish labeled "wild", and to avoid consuming too much mercury, eat small fish like sardines and anchovies. Finally, eliminate completely, or eat little of, the fatty or processed meats like hot dogs, cold cuts, bacon, salami, and so on. These meats contain too much fat and salt. Also, their nutritional value is low.

Good fat — To get healthy amounts of good fat, use olive, canola, or coconut oil to cook. Lean meats, chicken, and fish have healthy amounts of good fat, and so do nuts. In addition, dairy products like butter, sour cream, cottage cheese, and milk provide you with fat, but use them in moderation.

Eliminate or minimize eating out — Although much information and education exist in the area of healthy nutrition, eating out regularly has become customary in most developed countries, and the United States is not an exception. What is most damaging to our health is the habit of frequently consuming fast food, or prepackaged, processed, and precooked food.

> "Although the United States is the most powerful nation on earth, the one area in which this country does not excel is health. And the future is not bright. Almost a third of our young children are obese, and many do not exercise. No matter how much information becomes available about the dangers of a sedentary life and a diet heavily dependent on processed foods, we do not change our ways . . . While high-quality nutrition is available throughout the United States, the American public, rich and poor, is drawn to eating unhealthy food."
>
> — Dr. Joel Fuhrman,
> *Eat to Live*

This is a cultural aspect that needs to change in this country, but because it involves freedom of choice, economics, and systemic social change, I do not think this will happen soon. It keeps coming back to us as individuals. Society as a whole has become one of speed and convenience, and self-created stress. Most people, especially the middle class, seem to always be in a hurry.

One complaint I hear frequently from clients with whom I work is that they feel too stressed and tired. They spend all day working and taking care of their children, taking them to games, school events, and participating in other civic activities. They claim they do not have time to prepare meals at home, and most of the time they end up eating fast food or at a restaurant on their way back home. Many find themselves in a vicious cycle of trying to live the good life, but in the process, they are shortening their life span.

When you learn to consistently be relaxed through relaxation and meditation and you improve the way you feed your body, you will feel much better, you will even lose some pounds, but most of all, you will notice the improvement in your level of energy, your emotional moods, and your level of alertness and endurance to face the demands of your life in good health.

Movement and exercise — The human body is designed for frequent and consistent movement. Regrettably, modern life offers so much convenience, such as elevators, escalators, automobiles, chairs, and home delivery, which keeps the body from getting the physical stimulus it needs. Physical inactivity is a contributor to poor circulation, sluggish and stiff muscles and joints, and improper oxygenation of the muscles and other tissue.

Physical activity plays an important role in maintaining good levels of energy, stress management, and healing from many diseases. Exercise is recommended to everyone. It is part of a healthy lifestyle. It is also an important part of recovery from illness. Exercise is routinely recommended to patients suffering from a variety of illnesses, such as depression, anxiety, arthritis, cancer, diabetes, and heart disease, and has been shown to be effective. Intuitively we know that exercise helps us feel better when done consistently. We also know that exercise helps us control stress, lose weight, tone the muscles of the body, and improve our self-esteem.

The positive effects of exercise are of two types: physical and psychosocial. Some of the physical effects are improved brain functioning, greater production of endorphins that reduce pain and stress, and increased body temperature, which improves metabolism and encourages detoxification of the body.

Some of the psychosocial benefits of physical exercise are increased motivation and self-esteem. When you exercise regularly, you become more capable of performing daily tasks. Your emotional states improve, and you tend to develop more and better social interactions.

Movement and exercise enhance the mind-body-spirit connection. The mind, body, and spirit work together as a system; thus, the psychotherapeutic use of movement and exercise furthers the emotional, cognitive, physical, and societal integration of you as an individual. Please see the References list at the end of the book under "Physical Exercise" to find an exercise type and routine you may enjoy practicing.

YOUR SPIRIT — YOUR DIVINE ASPECT

I will discuss this component of your holistic existence in two ways: your emotional states and your spiritual beliefs.

Your emotional states — Your emotions reflect your spiritual state. Think about it. The word "inspire" has as its root the word "spirit." To be inspired means to be in spirit. Therefore, positive emotions reflect being in good spirit, and negative emotions such as anger and depression, and even milder negative emotions, reflect a negative emotional/spiritual state.

Using mind-body techniques improves your life physically and emotionally. They teach you to recognize when you are experiencing negative emotions, and help you bring yourself to a better emotional state quickly.

By the way, my Life Transformation Paradigm teaches you how to do this throughout the different chapters in this book. You will also learn two additional techniques at the end of this chapter.

Your spiritual beliefs — Your spiritual beliefs, whatever they are, are a foundation of your existence. Many people in the self-help arena are attempting to improve their lives and becoming better people by focusing on their patterns of thinking and their bodies through exercise and nutrition.

People who believe in a spiritual philosophy for living life need to also develop and strengthen their spiritual beliefs and practices. If you are already actively growing in your spirituality you can skip this section, or you can read it and perhaps you may be able to incorporate the practice I will share with you at the end of this chapter.

Most philosophies teach the concept of faith, trust, and life after death. I will share with you a meditation technique I use at the end of this chapter to strengthen my faith and my trust in God, and to gain the certainty that I will pass on to a better life than the life I have here on Earth. I am Catholic and my spiritual beliefs are Christian; therefore, I will share the meditation technique using Christian principles from the Bible. You can also adapt the technique to your own beliefs if they are not Christian.

CONCLUSION

The fifth lifestyle shift to live a happy, healthy, long, and prosperous life adds the dimension of living in peace. Being able to develop and sustain living in mental, physical, and spiritual health and balance adds a dimension to your life that few people have. You live life in peace, feeling and knowing that your present life and the next are safe and secure regardless of any obstacles, problems, and adversities you face during your existence in this world.

Below are four meditation exercises to take care of yourself holistically — mind, body, and spirit.

MEDITATION EXERCISES FOR MIND-BODY-SPIRIT SELF-CARE

Disputing and Changing Limiting Beliefs

This technique requires that you catch yourself when you start thinking limiting thoughts and immediately replace them with positive thoughts and expectations. Through this technique, you develop the habit of positive thinking and the attitude of self-confidence. This technique requires that you remain alert throughout the day about the kinds of thoughts and conversations you carry out with yourself, especially at times when things do not turn out the way you expected them.

The goal of the disputing limiting beliefs technique is to learn to change your train of negative thoughts as quickly as possible so you can change your physical and emotional states to positive ones immediately. This will help your brain function at peak capacity; otherwise, the longer you dwell in your negative and limiting thinking, the worse you will do in your learning and functioning as a human being. The idea is to catch yourself quickly and immediately turn your thinking into positive, hopeful, faithful thinking. This ability comes with repeated practice until it becomes a natural habit. Until it becomes an automatic habit, you need to do it in steps.

Here are the steps in the disputing limiting beliefs process:

1. **CHECK** — Check your thoughts frequently. Is what you are thinking limiting, negative, or doubtful? Notice how your thoughts make you feel in your body and your emotions. If you do not feel good or positive, you need to change your thoughts.

2. **STOP** — Once you determine that your thoughts need to be changed, tell yourself "Stop, I need to think positive about this situation." Speak to yourself with strength and assertiveness.

3. **BREATHE** — When you give yourself the command to stop, raise your head and take as many deep breaths as you need (usually four

or five) until you feel the tension being relieved, and tell yourself "I am replacing my negative thoughts with positive ones." Speak to yourself calmly and in an assertive tone.

4. **REPLACE** — Continue breathing deeply as you look up and talk positively to yourself about the problem, obstacle, or adversity you may be going through. Repeat this process throughout the day as you catch yourself dwelling in thoughts that are limiting or negative until it becomes automatic. It is important that you remain alert from now on and catch yourself when you are in a negative train of thought.

By the way, when you are trying to come up with positive thoughts, and your mind goes blank or wants to argue with you and take you back to negative or doubtful thinking, keep taking deep breaths and bring to your mind your vision for your future. This will generate thoughts of positive hope and expectation, and will bring to your mind additional positive thoughts.

As you become more aware and stay more alert about limiting and negative thoughts you will get better and more used to the disputing limiting beliefs process. Remember to:

1. **CHECK** — Check your thinking frequently.

2. **STOP** — Tell yourself "STOP!" when you catch yourself thinking limiting or negative thoughts.

3. **BREATHE** — Start and continue breathing deeply, slowly, and calmly.

4. **REPLACE** — Replace the negative thoughts with positive ones by looking up and continuing to breathe deeply, slowly, and calmly.

BODY HEALTH MEDITATIONS

Meditative Eating (Mindful Eating)

We have learned that nutrition is important in the management of stress and emotional states and in preventing and treating disease. Stress is aggravated by a hyperactive or busy lifestyle, negative emotional states, and unhealthy nutrition. Proper nutrition is important in the prevention of, and successful management of, chronic disease and unhealthy emotional states. A balanced nutritious diet is an important component of a mind-body-spirit program, and this is why it is included in this book.

Besides learning the basic nutrition principles in this program, it is important to learn the important skill called meditative or mindful eating. Mindful eating teaches you to appreciate food and to exercise control over food portions and develop healthier eating habits. Mindful eating can also be helpful for weight management and improving mental health.

It is interesting to note that even though people may be more aware of the importance of eating a healthier diet to remain healthy and for disease or weight management, most people are not aware of the importance of eating healthier for stress management and mental health. The intention in this chapter is to raise your awareness and motivate you to make improvements in your diet and eating, exercise habits, and spiritual practices in order to live a more holistic, systemic, and balanced life.

Mindful Eating — How It Is Done

Make time to be by yourself for this exercise. Have something relatively healthy for you to practice eating mindfully (fruit, vegetable, or a small salad). Make sure you can eat it by yourself, quietly and without interruptions.

1. Sit comfortably and relax by taking a few deep, relaxing breaths.

2. Appreciate your food for a couple of minutes. Be thankful for it and those who participated in the process to get it to your table, from growing it to preparing it so you can eat it.

3. Eat slowly — chew thoroughly, and taste and enjoy the food. Get all your senses involved.

4. Swallow and meditate — is the food nutritious? Is it good for your system, good for your health? Will it contribute to good or bad health? As you keep eating, stay focused on the food and enjoy it thoroughly. Think in silence only about the food.

5. Keep eating this way until you finish the food completely or at least for twenty minutes.

6. Once you have practiced for a while on your own, start eating your real meals mindfully.

7. Continue the practice at least one meal a day and three or four times a week. Engage others in the practice. With consistent practice, you will eat mindfully every time you consume food.

NOTE: By being mindful of your food and eating meditatively on a consistent basis, you become more aware of your present eating habits and you can gradually make changes and improvements to how you feed your body and your mind without struggle. You make changes more naturally and without struggling to make them.

BODY SCAN MEDITATION FOR BODY HEALTH

We will now practice mindfulness meditation using an exercise called a "body scan." This is a common way to begin the practice of mindfulness. The body scan meditation involves breathing deeply while allowing individual parts of your body to relax and experience stress reduction and a peaceful state. Practicing this meditation consistently helps you reduce stress when you practice it, and it conditions your mind and your body to automatically relax and remain more at peace when you face situations that would trigger negative emotions in you.

1. Please sit comfortably and begin breathing slowly and deeply like you have done before.

2. Relax and close your eyes, and just follow my directions as you continue being relaxed and at peace. I will guide you through a scan of your entire body one section at a time. As I mention each section and you place your attention on that section of your body and its parts, allow yourself to notice any sensations. If you notice sensations of discomfort, allow these parts of your body to relax, and imagine letting go of the discomfort with every relaxing breath you take. As you feel sensations of relaxation, health, and wellness, continue feeling these sensations with every breath you take.

3. Place your attention on your head and your entire face down to your neck. Take a deep breath and let your head, entire face, and neck relax deeply. Continue breathing deeply and relax more and more.

4. Now, notice your throat, shoulders, arms, and hands, down to your fingertips. Take a deep, relaxing breath, and allow your throat, shoulders, arms, and hands down to your fingertips to deeply relax. Continue breathing deeply and relax more and more.

5. Now notice your chest, heart, lungs, and your upper back. Take a deep, relaxing breath and allow your chest, heart, lungs, and your upper back to relax more and more. Continue breathing deeply and relax more and more.

6. Now, focus your attention on your stomach and midsection, including the middle of your back. Take a deep, relaxing breath and allow your stomach, entire midsection, and the middle of your back to relax deeply. Continue breathing deeply and relax more and more.

7. Now focus your attention on the lower part of your body, from your waist down. Notice the lower part down to the tip of your spinal cord and all the way down to your toes, including the soles of your feet. Take a deep breath and relax the entire lower part of your body all the way down to your feet, including the soles of both feet. Continue breathing deeply and allow yourself to relax more and more, and deeper and deeper.

8. Allow yourself to feel how relaxed your entire body is. Take five deep, relaxing breaths. This is the feeling of peace, health, and wellness.

9. Notice how relaxed you are in mind, body, and spirit. Bring your attention back to the room. Feel the chair you are sitting on and notice the room's environment: how cold or warm it is, the smells in the air, and any noises. Become more and more aware of the room as you slowly open your eyes. Take a long and deep energizing breath. Stand up and stretch your arms and your entire body and come back to your seat.

MIND-BODY-SPIRIT MEDITATION

Mind Conditioning

Mind conditioning is a subconscious learning procedure. We have done this before. This is a meditation which includes the power of four therapies. I will explain to you what happens in your brain in more detail. You will understand the science behind it and why it works.

I have used this intervention with many of my clients for many years and I have seen it change the lives of everyone who practices it consistently without exception. I strongly recommend it to develop new or better behaviors and to strengthen mindsets, as well as to induce healing from illnesses and medical interventions.

Practicing mind conditioning regularly will give you long-lasting benefits in any area of your life that you want to improve. We will use it here to help you develop a stronger certainty about making any goal or desire you decide to pursue a reality. The certainty within you that something you desire will come to pass is called faith and trust. I will guide you in practice and demonstration to apply mind conditioning to growing in faith and trust.

These are the steps or components of the process of mind conditioning:

Deep breathing — I have already explained what happens in your body and your brain when you practice deep breathing, but let me mention it again. With deep breathing, your blood circulation normalizes. Your vessels open up so that blood and oxygen can flow through them normally. This means you are allowing much more blood and oxygen to your entire brain and body, which translates to much better functioning of thinking, reasoning, memory, and comprehension, as well as much better emotional functioning. Remember that to take deep breaths correctly, you inhale slowly through your nose, hold the air in for a count of four or five seconds, and exhale slowly through your mouth.

Relaxing instrumental music — You can find many recordings on YouTube by searching "Relaxing and concentration music," or you can find music to download or CDs on Amazon by doing the same search.

Relaxing music is helpful in reducing stress and anxiety in our mind, body and spirit. Listening to this music naturally helps you relax even when you are under a lot of stress or pressure. Being able to stay calm and relaxed under pressure helps your brain stay focused on the task at hand as well as concentrate and avoid distractions, thus improving your health and increasing your learning and memory abilities.

Positive visualization — In this step, you visualize as detailed and vividly as you can the outcomes that you want. For example, in this practice exercise, you want to strengthen your faith and trust to develop the habit of feeling certain you can accomplish any goal, desire, or dream you decide to pursue. You can imagine yourself being strong and self-confident, and taking action to obtain your desire. You can visualize yourself having achieved your dream and living your life as you expect it to be when you achieve your goal. When you visualize, you need to put yourself in the picture and add color and action, just as if you were in a movie.

How does this help you? To the brain, what it physically and materially sees is almost the same as when it imagines it. Showing your vision to your brain in your imagination shows your brain how you want to be and what you want to accomplish with belief and positive feelings, making it think it is real. Your mind moves you in the direction of your dream, and to take actions that will turn it into reality.

Positive self-affirmation — Through deep breathing and the relaxing music, you achieve a state of mind which is receptive to understanding and recording new information in your brain. This state of mind is registered on instruments which monitor the brain electronically, and is called the alpha brain frequency (refer back to the brain wave descriptions in Chapter 2).

Many scientific experiments have been done that demonstrate that people can perform tasks much better and faster, heal easier and faster, and remember much greater amounts of information and with much better comprehension when the information has been studied in the alpha state. It stands to reason, then, that when you give your brain positive affirmations that reinforce what you are vividly visualizing while in the alpha state, this information will be strongly recorded in your memory, creating in your mind the new belief you want to develop much quicker.

HOW TO DO THE MIND CONDITIONING MEDITATION

Mind conditioning can be used to realize any desire, dream, or goal. In this section, I am introducing it to improve spiritually. You need to develop three to six short affirmations that have personal meaning to you. Once you develop your affirmations, you can continue using them each time you repeat the meditation, or you can also change them periodically as often as you need.

What I recommend is starting with three affirmations and over time add the other three to bring the affirmations up to the maximum of six.

Your affirmations should be short and in the present tense, as if the outcomes you want were already part of your present life experience. For example, I stated earlier that as a demonstration, I would make my desire one of having faith that gives me the conviction that everything I want to come into my life will happen if I decide to pursue it.

Faith is a spiritual value taught by most spiritual philosophies. In the Contemporary English Version of the Bible is a verse on what faith is, known by most Christians — Hebrews 11:1. It reads like this: "Faith makes us sure of what we hope for and gives us proof of what we cannot see." This is the kind of faith I would like to develop to help myself gain certainty and dispel doubt about my goals, dreams, and desires.

Here are six affirmations I would write based on this Bible quote:

- I am totally certain I can achieve all the desires I decide to pursue.

- I have successfully achieved other goals; therefore, I know I will succeed again.

- I see the proof that others have been successful at achieving this dream; therefore, I too can achieve it.

- I am sure I can achieve this desire.

- I am totally certain of the positive outcome I want.

- In my mind, my dream is already reality.

NOTE: You can also include the Bible quote as an affirmation if it helps you connect strongly with what faith is. Personally, I would use the Bible affirmation as the first and last and include four affirmations from the ones I listed above.

1. Start playing relaxing instrumental music at a volume comfortable to you.

2. Sit comfortably with your feet flat on the floor and your back flat against the back of a comfortable chair. Let your arms rest over your lap and keep your head straight as if you were looking straight forward and gently close your eyes.

3. Start taking deep, relaxing breaths. Inhale through your nose slowly. Breathe into your stomach, not into your chest, and let your stomach expand as you breathe in. Hold the air in for a mental count of five seconds, and exhale through your mouth slowly. Continue breathing this way through the exercise.

4. Continue taking slow, deep, relaxing breaths as you listen to the music and notice the calming effect it has on you.

5. Start visualizing yourself as the person full of faith and certainty to achieve every dream you decide to follow. Visualize yourself taking actions and steps to obtain your dream. See yourself already living your dream and feeling great for having achieved it. Remember to continue breathing deeply and relaxing through the process of visualizing.

6. Continue breathing deeply and remaining relaxed, and begin repeating your affirmations as you continue visualizing the outcomes your affirmations represent for you. Repeat each affirmation three times to yourself quietly or in silence. State each

repetition slowly so you can experience what they mean with positive emotions.

7. Conclude the meditation by remaining in silence for three to five minutes, or longer if you desire. After this time, slowly open your eyes and stretch your body as you remain seated, and then get up and stretch a bit more. When you feel more energy and more physically active, you can continue with the activities of your day.

Perform this meditation at least once every day for four to six weeks, preferably twice a day. The time of day to practice it should be when it is comfortable for you. You will notice changes within you such as greater motivation, more courage and certainty in your thinking, and improvements in your well-being.

Mind conditioning is a powerful meditation to create personal change and to achieve your goals, desires, and dreams.

Living is holistic and systemic. Take care of your mind, body, and spirit.

SUCCESS IS FOR EVERYONE

Success is meant for everyone, not just for a chosen few.
Success can be achieved by anyone. Success is meant for you.
Before you can achieve success, you must know what it is.
Before you can believe it, you must know what it means.

Success to most means money and recognition. It is deceiving.
Only few people know that true success is a style of living.
Success is peace of mind, to be content with what you have,
but always trying to do better for the benefit of man.

Success is feeling good about yourself regardless of events.
Success is energy and motivation to always do the best you can.
Success is faith, hope, and optimism when times are tough.
Success is lifting others up when they are having it rough.

Success is having discipline to take good care of yourself.
Success is best enjoyed when you are in good physical health.
Success is not indulging in what you know is bad and harmful.
If you mistreat your body, success for you is doubtful.

Success is having sincere loving relationship and friendships.
Success is not being seen by others as a superficial fool.
Success is honesty, fairness, integrity, and appreciation.
Success is being an example of living by the Golden Rule.

Few people find true success. We look in the wrong places.
We keep looking for it in money, people, things, and places.
Only few find the right source; most still like the deceiving.
Only a few know that success is a balanced
mind-body-spirit style of living.

— **Jose M. Baltazar, PhD**

CHAPTER 8

Lifestyle Shift #6: Optimism—Emotions Are Critical

"This expanded model of what it means to be 'intelligent' puts emotions at the center of aptitudes for living. These abilities, (Emotional Intelligence), can preserve our most prized relationships, or their lack corrode them . . . and toxic emotions put our physical health at as much risk as does chain smoking, even as emotional balance can help protect our health and well-being."

— Dr. Daniel Goleman, *Emotional Intelligence: Why It Can Matter More Than IQ* (parentheses mine)

MY FATHER WAS AN OPTIMIST

I have never taken an IQ test, but I would venture to say that if I took one, I probably would not score high—and yet I can tell you with truth and certainty that I have accomplished all of my dreams and goals. I am financially independent and live a happy and fulfilling life. By schooling standards, I am an educated person. I hold four college degrees and numerous certifications that require lots of study and preparation to get them. I have received numerous awards and recognitions in my profession, and I am a trainer of other professionals. I love learning and contributing to the lives of others through what I learn.

I share this with you because you are a person who is looking for ways to improve your life (you would not be reading this book if you were not). I do not share it to boost my ego but to tell you that I am an average person who struggled a lot through school. Now that I am educated on the brain and how it works, psychology, and mind-body medicine, I know that optimism was one of the main factors that pulled me through school and life successfully.

I learned optimism from my father. I owe my optimistic attitude to him. My parents lived in Mexico most of their lives. I lived in Mexico until the age of 15. My father was always a small business owner. As far as I can remember, we relocated to three different states in Mexico. Wherever we lived, my father was a small grocery store owner. He would set up his store from scratch each time, and immediately he would start generating sales and income that provided our family a middle-class lifestyle.

My dad used to have me help him tend the store after school hours, and this experience helped me understand how he thought about running his business, and how he walked his talk. I remember relatives and friends would ask my dad how he did it when he became profitable so quickly. His answers used to be Mexican folk sayings. He would say *"Hasta para ser huevón se tiene que usar la mente,"* (Even to be lazy requires thinking) or the traditional Spanish equivalent of "Early to bed, early to rise makes a man healthy, wealthy, and wise" (*Al que madruga Dios le ayuda*). I learned quite a few of these sayings from him and saw him live them; now I live my life by many of these sayings.

One of the foundational characteristics of optimism is that of emotional intelligence, and one of the foundational characteristics of emotional intelligence is the ability to calm yourself down quickly when you find yourself in adversity or under pressure. My father used to be able to do this. I saw him practice it many times throughout his life, and every time, I saw him solve difficult situations successfully.

One experience that remains fresh in my mind took place when I was 11 years old. A huge supermarket opened one block away from his store. Everyone, including my mom and sisters, used to tell my dad he was not going to be able to compete with it. I used to hear it so frequently that even I suggested moving away. Instead of panicking, here is the saying I remember my dad telling me: "*Si vamos a caber en el cielo.*" "If we're all going to fit in heaven, *there is space for the big market and my store here.*" (I added the italics to show what in this case the saying meant to me.) I saw him being able to relax and continue to take his daily nap and sleep like an angel. My mother used to say, "I don't know how he's able to sleep when the store may be going broke real soon!"

After a couple of weeks, he came up with the answers to this situation. His solutions to the problem were:

1. Open earlier than the supermarket and cater to people who needed to buy products earlier than the supermarket's opening time.

2. Close two hours later than the supermarket.

3. Keep his store and products cleaner and more organized than the supermarket.

4. Offer free transportation and delivery to customers buying groceries for the week. (This was an innovation at that time. The supermarkets did not offer this service back then.)

5. He somehow negotiated lower wholesale prices for many essential products from his suppliers, thus being able to sell at lower prices than the supermarket.

6. He hired a clerk to help him during the additional open hours and with deliveries.

The supermarket owners implemented my father's idea of free transportation and delivery, and he saw this as an opportunity to meet with the owners. He became friends with the owners, and they helped each other succeed by cooperating with each other instead of getting into a competition war. Five years later, my dad sold his successful store. He needed a change. My mom was a U.S. citizen and, as everyone says, "We came to the United States to pursue the American Dream."

OPTIMISM IS NOT AN EMOTION

Living in optimism is a part of my Life Transformation Paradigm model because optimism plays an important role in the quality of our lives. Optimism is not an emotion. It is a logical and critical thinking process that, when practiced, leads us to think more rationally and logically. Thinking optimistically helps us make choices and actions that are more likely to produce the results we want which, in turn, take us to experience a lifestyle filled with positivism and emotional balance.

Being optimistic is usually equated with positive thinking. Positive thinking is one component of optimism. However, optimistic thinking goes beyond positive thinking, as you will see in this chapter.

THE OPTIMISTIC LIFESTYLE

The optimistic lifestyle is based on positive psychology made popular by Dr. Martin Seligman. Dr. Seligman has conducted perhaps the most scientific research on the subject of optimism. He shares his research in his book *Learned Optimism*. He has discovered that optimistic people are much more prosperous than pessimistic people.

Prosperity is not measured or demonstrated only by material affluence, although this is one indicator. Through his research, Dr. Seligman has demonstrated that optimistic people are happier and live more rewarding lives than pessimistic individuals. Other characteristics are that they live longer, they are healthier, they enjoy better and happier relationships, they do better in school, they get jobs faster, they have higher salaries, and they get promoted more often than pessimistic people.

The amazing thing that he has discovered is that optimistic people are not necessarily more intelligent than pessimistic people as demonstrated by IQ tests and other kinds of tests, such as SAT and ACT tests. There are pessimistic people with high IQs and they do terrible in school and life, and there are optimistic people with average IQs who do great in school and life.

My dad only went to second grade in school and yet was successful in most areas of his life. I have also worked with many clients who in their thinking are pessimistic. After I work with them and teach them processes to develop optimism, they start adapting a more optimistic style of thinking and they have been able to accomplish much more than they thought they were capable of accomplishing.

Optimism is a state of mind, and it also is a style of life. Now I understand why I, with such an average intellectual intelligence, have been able to achieve all of my goals and desires. When I look back and take inventory of my own life, I realize that everything I have desired to accomplish has become a reality for me. I learned to keep an optimistic attitude from my father. He was one of the most optimistic people I ever knew. He taught me not to let adversity and obstacles bring me down emotionally, and instead remain calm, cool, and collected, to look for solutions to problems in a calm and cool state of mind, and find the positive in every circumstance even when things seem to be going badly.

THE BIOLOGY OF OPTIMISM

How does optimism affect our learning and quality of life? We are born to learn from life experience. Each of us is constantly learning whether we realize it or not (remember the chapter on awareness). Our attitudes, values, and beliefs determine the kind of learning that takes effect within us. Learning is a self-reinforcing cycle. The quality of our attitudes, values, and beliefs reinforces the quality of learning that takes place within us. Good-quality attitudes, values, and beliefs produce the same type of learning. Bad-quality attitudes, values, and beliefs produce bad learning.

Our brain is our learning computer, and our attitudes, values, and beliefs are recorded in it. Our brain is divided into two hemispheres and both sides communicate with each other through the corpus collosum, a thick network of cells that joins both sides of the brain and serves as the channel of communication between them. Communication between the two sides of the brain is always happening; therefore, what each side registers and processes affects the other.

A foundational concept of the brain is that the right side of the brain manages emotions and the left manages logic. Since both sides of the brain communicate with each other, and this communication is always happening, it makes sense that the quality of our emotions will have an effect on the left side of the brain (the logical side). Therefore, if your emotions are positive, the left side of the brain will be affected positively; thus, good learning will take place because the left side of the brain will also work much better when your emotions are positive.

Optimism is not an emotion. It is a learned, logic-driven behavior. However, all positive emotions stem from optimism. For example, instances of anger occur to most of us at one point or another in our lives. Optimism helps you recover quicker from anger or any other negative emotion.

The pessimistic person will allow the negative emotion to take over and linger for as long as his mind keeps focusing on the emotion — in this example, the emotion of anger or the incident that caused the anger. The optimistic person consciously or subconsciously has learned to calm down and, through logical self-talk and actions, dispels the bad sensations from his body and talks himself out of continuing to feel angry. Now, you tell me: which of the two reactions is better? Which one will cause your mind or brain to function much better, feel more tranquil, keep you healthier, and think more clearly?

Optimism goes beyond keeping a positive attitude regardless of circumstances. A positive mental attitude is good. Optimism adds another dimension to keeping a positive mental attitude at all times. Optimism adds self-evaluation, evaluation of the circumstances, and more accurate decisions and actions. These are logical functions of the left side of the brain which require that positive emotions, which are a function of the right side of the brain, be reasonable and balanced. Even positive euphoria, although it is a positive emotion, because of its extreme sensation of good feeling, causes the left side not to function properly while you are in a state of extreme excitement. You have to calm yourself down to a more reasonable state of happiness for better reasoning.

Below is a chart that shows attitudes and behaviors of optimistic and pessimistic people. See which ones you identify with the most. Although this is not a scientific test, it points out areas in which you can become more optimistic. Later in this chapter, you will learn practical ways by which you can improve your optimism, even if you are already optimistic.

Optimism:

- You look forward to another day of life and make it as enjoyable as possible because your daily activity and responsibilities help you get what you want for your life. You feel in control of your life.

- You look forward to the challenges of the day. Even though it means work and effort, you appreciate the value of facing them. Getting through the challenges causes you to feel intelligent and accomplished.

- You often think about your future with positive expectations and hope.

- You have goals that are important to you, and you pursue them with the expectation of accomplishing them.

- You feel certain that in one way or another, you contribute daily to the good of others.

- You are certain that you can solve any problem that faces you.

- When you talk about your dreams with others, your conversations are more focused on what you expect to pursue and accomplish.

- When you think about your life, you expect to get the good things you desire.

Pessimism:

- There are areas in your life which you want to improve, but you have resigned yourself to your present condition rather than trying.

- When new ideas are presented to you, you tend to shut them down.

- When you do something wrong, you feel guilty for a long time.

- When you attempt to do something and it does not turn out the way you expect it to, your disappointment lasts for a long time.

- When you consider trying out new ideas or actions, you demotivate yourself by focusing more on the obstacles than the benefits.

- Your internal dialogue (self-talk) is mostly focused on the negative aspects of your life rather than on the positive conditions you have.

- You feel you are doing many things because you have to and not because you want to.

- You spend a lot of time wishing things were different in your life, but you are doing little or nothing to change them.

- When you discuss your dreams with others, your conversation is more focused on problems and obstacles than on the positive results of obtaining it.

These statements point out if you tend to be more pessimistic than optimistic or the other way around. But in any case, you can always become more optimistic to help your brain function better logically and emotionally.

Just like in the other chapters, I will share with you three techniques to get you started making this shift in your life.

Optimism, along with the other shifts, works as a system that will help you live a healthy, happy, long, and prosperous life without stress. You will live the life you are designed to live.

STRATEGIES TO GROW IN OPTIMISM

Subconscious Decision-Making/Problem-Solving

I learned this process from my father. He never gave this habit an official name. I coined the name as a result of my studies in psychology, mind-body medicine, and accelerated learning.

My father used to tell me, "You don't gain anything by losing sleep over a problem; relax instead, and be thankful for being alive." When my father was going through a rough experience, he would lie down and fall asleep—just as he did when things were fine—and took his usual nap. My mom would ask how he could take naps as if nothing were happening. My dad would answer her with the expression above. I would wonder also, but as I developed the ability to relax and, yes, sleep well even when times were rough, I found that when I am awake, I can think better and clearer. Too many people spend too much time worrying about problems, and this affects the ability of their brains to perform well in other areas where they need to continue functioning normally, such as critical thinking and problem-solving.

Because optimism is a habit of thinking, and thinking translates to behavior, in order to improve our thinking, we need to continuously remind ourselves of the new thinking and attempt to act accordingly until it becomes a habit. Now, the idea of this strategy is not necessarily to be able to sleep; this is one way my father manifested this thinking. The idea is to minimize worrying and get rid of obsessive negative, worrisome thinking when you find yourself going through bad experiences.

Here are the steps to subconscious decision-making and problem-solving:

1. Frequently through the day, repeat to yourself the phrase "I don't gain anything by worrying. I can think better if I relax."

2. Make time to relax by yourself. Find a quiet place and get away from the hustle and bustle. Practice deep breathing as you have learned in previous chapters. Relax with deep breaths until you feel tranquil and at peace.

3. In that relaxed and quiet state, simply ask yourself: what is the best response or action to take in whatever rough situation or important decision you are trying to make? Continue relaxing. Eventually, sooner rather than later, you will get an impression, feeling, or sense of direction as to what to do. Once you get an answer, write it down and carry out that action.

Your subconscious is your best guide. Your subconscious has the answer or solution to any situation you face. Deep relaxation is the best way to reach your deeper wisdom. With practice, you can get access to your subconscious for answers about any area in your life.

Disputing Adverse Events

When you find yourself facing some form of problem, obstacle, or adversity, the following strategies help you reduce the stress and anxiety and help refocus your energy and attention to find solutions to bad events in your life.

1. *There is always someone who has it worse than you.* Whenever you are going through a negative experience, take a few deep breaths and relax. When you are relaxed, realize that there are other people in worse circumstances than you and be thankful for what

you have. This does not mean that you get all happy and joyous about the worse situation of someone else. It means that there are other people to be concerned about. You raise your sensitivity and empathy for others, thus helping you realize that your situation is not the only bad situation. When this happens, you become grateful that you are not doing as badly.

2. Gratefulness is a spiritual state and thus can be better experienced in a state of meditation. Therefore, just like in other exercises in this book, the next step is to relax deeply and meditate on what you have for which you are grateful. Think of as many things you can, and express sincere gratitude to God, yourself, and any other entity or person who has made it possible for you to be in a better situation than many others. In addition, send good intentions to those having it worse than you.

Being thankful for what you have calms you down and frees your mind from the negative emotions you may be feeling. You will be able to think clearer and come up with alternative actions to take or alternative solutions to your problem.

This is the miracle of optimism. Am I saying that you should not feel bad about the bad situation you are in? No — what is bad is feeling bad for a long time or allowing it to sink you into sadness, anger, disappointment, confusion, or desperation for a long time. These are disempowering emotions and one of the reasons most people do not realize their higher desires or goals.

The key to this technique is to be aware of negative emotions caused by negative circumstances. Consciously take time to think and realize that others have it worse than you, and consciously be thankful that although circumstances are not perfect, you have it better than others. Eventually this way of thinking becomes a habit, and you do it automatically. You come up with better solutions when you remain optimistic, because your brain functions much better.

Adjust and Adapt

The great teacher and author Dr. Wayne Dyer used to say, "When you change the way you look at things, the things you look at change." How you perceive things makes a big difference as to whether you persist or give up when you are trying to reach a higher goal or desire. If you give up or get discouraged too soon, you show symptoms of a pessimistic personality. If you focus on what is displeasing or inconvenient, you will stop trying too soon and you will also give up.

Winston Churchill's phrase "Never, never, never give up!" is an imperative that optimistic people practice.

To continue trying, one of the best things to do is to adapt and adjust. This is a characteristic of optimistic people. Optimistic people do not insist on circumstances or life adjusting to what they consider to be "the way." Instead, they adjust their plans and their thinking to better fit the situation at hand so they can find ways to dig under, go around it, or climb over it. Pessimistic people tend to see the world in a set way, and they find it hard to change thinking that the world must change around them instead of them changing with the world.

Below are practical steps by which you can adjust and adapt when circumstances are not favorable, and yet it is better to go through and come out successful because succeeding through them gets you closer to your goal:

1. **Relax and assess the circumstances.** Find a quiet place and take a few deep breaths until you feel relaxed. Think about how getting through this successfully gets you one step closer to your vision, your dream, your goal. Motivate yourself by focusing on what you expect to accomplish instead of the present circumstances. Visualize in your mind the positive future you want.

2. **Burn your bridges.** Make the decision and develop the habit of finishing something once you start on it. This does not mean necessarily that you will do or die, but it does mean that you

realize that anything worthwhile will have its problems. If you start thinking about giving up too soon or settling for easier alternatives when problems start, the probability of failing is high.

3. **Look for help early.** Many people wait until it is too late before getting help. Others never look or ask for it. They give up, thinking that there is nothing else they can do. Instead, as soon as you notice that there are problems, or that your efforts are not working well, you should look and ask for help. Talk to your friends and family, a professional coach, a role model, or someone who has gone through a similar experience. Do not exclude anyone that can be helpful. You never know what ideas they can give you or what help they may provide to you.

4. **Live life on the optimistic side.** In his book *Authentic Happiness*, Dr. Martin E.P. Seligman discusses how happy people are able to keep developing their virtues. One recommendation he makes is to commit yourself to doing something every day that reinforces virtues that you already hold or that you are trying to develop. He suggests that you journal each day about your experience. What did you do? How did you feel when you did it?

Here is what one lady shared in one of my workshops after she decided to journal for a week. She shared that although she considers herself a loving mother (her virtue), she decided to more intentionally do something loving for her children every day for two weeks. When she came back to continue my series of workshops, she shared that although she always does loving things for her children, the experience of being more mindful about it and journaling on it every day was an enriching experience. It brought her closer to her children, and it has made her more aware of how much they need her love and attention.

Does this sound optimistic to you? I am sure it does. You see, it is not that she did not do loving things for her children; she did.

It is the heightened level of awareness that has raised her level of happiness and optimism about her children.

I practice this process on my goals. My virtue is that I am committed to achieving my goals. Committing to do something towards achieving them every single day and journaling about it in the evening keeps my level of commitment high every day even when things do not go well. I remain optimistic and hopeful for the next day.

Give this practice a try — if not to obtain a higher dream, to enrich your present life.

Optimism is a powerful attitude and skill. By now, if you have been practicing some, or even better, all of the techniques offered to you in this book, you have already improved your optimism significantly. All the techniques have the purpose of helping your mind (brain) function much better by training you to behave in more positive and optimistic ways.

> "When you change the way you look at things, the things you look at change."
>
> — Dr. Wayne Dyer

ATTITUDES OF OPTIMISM

Success and happiness for most are hard to find.
They don't know it's all in the state of mind.
Your success and happiness depend on your attitudes —
for you see, your attitudes will always determine your altitude.

Develop positive attitudes towards life.
Learn to be positive even in the roughest of times.
Learn to see what you have left instead of what you lack.
This attitude will keep you going. It will pull you up.

Smile at life and people even when times are bad.
Learn to find good reasons for living even when life is rough.
Learn to expect good from the future even when
the present is dark.
These attitudes are so positive that positive things they attract.

Learn to think good of yourself even when others hurt you.
Always consider yourself a valuable person.
This is healthy, I tell you. Accept your mistakes
and grow from them instead of becoming sour.
These attitudes build you up. They give personal power.

Get rid of the negative attitudes of anger, fear, and pessimism.
These attitudes produce unhappiness, failure,
and unhealthy pressure.
Replace them with love, hope, faith, and optimism,
and success and happiness will follow,
and life will give you its treasure.

— Dr. Jose M. Baltazar

CHAPTER 9

Lifestyle Shift #7: Total Responsibility— Live by Choice, Not by Chance

YOUR LIFE IS THE SUM OF YOUR CHOICES

Almost everyone understands the meaning of phrases like "Your life is the sum of your choices," "Every action creates an equal and opposite reaction," "Every choice has a consequence," and so on. Even so, it seems as though many people forget about these truisms. Too many of us end up making wrong choices, yet everyone deals differently with the outcomes of the choice, and everyone learns differently from the experience.

No one is exempt from making mistakes and wrong decisions. What makes the difference among people is how they deal with the mistake or outcome from the bad decision. There are different ways of dealing with the outcomes of a wrong choice. The way people deal with a bad choice reflects how much responsibility they are taking for the choice and its outcomes. This is the topic of this chapter.

The seventh lifestyle shift in my Life Transformation Paradigm model is called "Total Responsibility: Live by Choice, not by Chance." The overall message in it is that by living life being totally responsible for their choices, a person can learn better from the experience and can make better adjustments and course corrections in their life. By resorting to blaming, justifying, or being rescued, learning is obstructed, and the likelihood of making another bad choice increases in probability and frequency.

Total responsibility lifestyle is supported by a psychological therapy approach called reality and choice theory.

WHY DO WE BEHAVE THE WAY WE DO?

Reality and Choice Theory Therapy

Dr. William Glasser is a psychiatrist known worldwide for developing a system of psychotherapy based on personal choice and brain functioning. The original name of his therapeutic approach was named "reality therapy," and in his landmark book by the same title he explains and documents why reality therapy is effective. Reality therapy has been in existence since the 1960s. Throughout the years and with more extensive research into reality therapy and neuroscience, Dr. Glasser renamed his method "choice theory" in 1996.

Dr. Glasser's foundational premise for his therapy is that people act the way they do because they are always attempting to fulfill a personal need. Every choice and every action a person takes is an attempt to fulfill one or both of the two foundational needs common to every human being: one, the need to love and be loved, and two, the need to feel that we are worthwhile to ourselves and to others.

According to Dr. Glasser, all behaviors are driven by the need to satisfy these needs. Good and bad behaviors, as dictated by society, are the result of attempting to fulfill these basic needs. When a person exhibits unacceptable behavior, his intention is the same as a person who exhibits acceptable behavior. Both are attempting to satisfy one or both of the two foundational needs. Dr. Glasser refers to bad behaviors as out-of-reality behaviors because they lead to negative and adverse results. Good and acceptable behaviors are reality behaviors because they lead to better and more realistic outcomes, thus the name reality therapy.

The goal of reality therapy is to help people who exhibit wrong behaviors move to the side of reality which is displayed in better choices and actions. For an individual who exhibits wrong behaviors, to be able to improve her life, she must first accept responsibility for her behavior and her life.

The second foundational principle of reality therapy is that of responsibility. People who misbehave must accept responsibility for their own choices and actions. "The devil made me do it" is not acceptable in reality therapy because even if a person was misguided by someone, he made the choice — even if it was made unintentionally or in a state of ignorance. This acceptance of total responsibility for all his choices empowers the individual to learn and become wiser.

In 1996, Dr. Glasser renamed his approach to counseling and psychotherapy choice theory. That same year, he published his famous book *Choice Theory: A New Psychology of Personal Freedom*. The underlying principles are the same as reality therapy; however, in choice theory, he expands the number of needs that drive people to make the choices they make to five and includes research on brain functioning to explain further how people become motivated to behave in ways that, in their thinking, will help them meet their needs.

The five needs that drive people to behave the way they do are survival, love and belonging, power, freedom, and fun. We are always behaving in a way that we feel or think will be able to meet the most predominant need or needs at any particular time. For example, I am writing this book right now because completing it and publishing it will fulfill my need for love (desire to serve others), power (I want to be a recognized author), and fun (I enjoy writing on topics that help other people). However, in a few minutes, I will stop writing and will watch with attention a movie I like and I know I will enjoy. My need for fun by entertainment is taking higher priority than my need for power, love, and having fun writing. It is important to me to finish writing the book, but at this point I decided to postpone the completion of my book by my choice to watch the movie.

I have used this simple example to illustrate how I arrived at my choice of watching the movie instead of continuing to write my book. Let us look at a bigger real-life situation to understand behavior and resolve issues the reality/choice theory way.

Reality/Choice Theory and My Life Transformation Paradigm Model Applied

One of my initial conversations with clients at the beginning of my coaching sessions is to make them aware that I will not be directing them as to what they should do to resolve the issue for which I am being consulted. I will serve as a source of information and as a guide to help them come up with alternatives, from which they can make choices as to what actions are most helpful to them to resolve the issue(s) they want to solve. They need to understand that they are responsible for finding the solution to their problem. I am a facilitator to assist them in the process.

Many therapists, counselors, and coaches tell their clients what actions to take to resolve a problem or issue they are facing. Using a directive approach opens up the opportunity to blame the coach if the recommendation given does not work for the client. Under the total responsibility principle of my coaching model, and the teachings of reality therapy and choice theory, the coach becomes a facilitator to the client for making his own decisions. If the choice made by the client does not work, he knows he decided it and he can make a different choice of action. The self-questioning process I share with you below is an effective model to use by yourself.

In the following section, I will share with you an actual case in which I used all components of my model for you to see how it can be used in real life. You will recognize how I use each component to guide my client to develop his own solution to his issue. In addition, I document for you three procedures I used within the total responsibility component to help this client arrive at his own solution. These three procedures can be useful to you in resolving any issues you need to solve, now or in the future.

MY MODEL IN ACTION — PUTTING IT ALL TOGETHER

I worked with a young man and his grandmother. I will name him Robert to keep his real name confidential. Robert was sixteen years old and living with his grandmother. His dad lived out of town and his mom, a single mother, suffered from mental illness and could not take care of him. Robert was experiencing problems in school. He was not applying himself to his studies, and his grades were getting worse. He was in danger of not being promoted to his senior year in high school, graduating late, or not graduating at all.

It turns out Robert was going through emotional stress due to his family situation. He wanted to live in a normal family situation — by normal, he meant to live with one of his parents since they were divorced. He was not able to fulfill his need of being loved and of belonging, even though his grandmother was doing her best to help him live a normal life as much as she could. The other needs he was not seeing fulfilled were those for power and freedom, since he could not decide for himself with whom to live. He was feeling demotivated and depressed, so he was not having any fun, either.

Robert's grandmother was at a loss. She did not know what else to try or do, and now they were having trouble in their relationship. Typical of relationships in trouble, the blame game was at a high level. They were blaming each other for the state of affairs. Blaming is a typical reaction when people find themselves in trouble. The following is the plan of action I followed to help Robert deal with his issue:

1. Teach him and his grandmother simple relaxation and medita-tion techniques so they could consistently reduce the stress levels in their lives and their relationship.

2. Help Robert regain his self-confidence and self-belief by helping him focus on his previous experiences of success as a student, and how he and his grandmother used to keep their relationship successful.

3. Help Robert clarify his future by helping him internalize what he would gain by doing well in school and what he would lose by failing to graduate from high school and college.

4. Help both of them internalize the importance of their relationship and how keeping a good relationship between them contributed to their happiness, their need to love and be loved, and their individual well-being and happiness.

5. Make nutritional, exercise, and meditation recommendations to improve physical energy and facilitate positive moods.

6. Help Robert clarify the choices he was making and whether they contributed to or hindered his school performance, well-being, future success, and self-empowerment.

Both learned to be more positive and optimistic about life through the process and interventions I taught them.

Some interventions I used working with Robert were the same I have included in each chapter of this book. Below, I explain how I helped Robert understand the concept of choice and total responsibility and include three additional interventions I taught him regarding being totally responsible for resolving his issue.

TOTAL RESPONSIBILITY AND CHOICE

When I consult with clients, they will always express in their own language the need(s) they are not able to meet. This opens the door for discussing the subject of making choices that take them further away or get them closer to get what they need. In the case of Robert, what he needed most was to satisfy the need for power and the need for freedom. He felt powerless not having the freedom to decide with whom to live. His relationship with his grandmother was deteriorating, and his motivation to do well in school and in life was declining due to the strain on the relationship.

After clarifying with him that his needs were power and freedom, I had him think and write about what choices he could make that would help him feel he had more freedom and more power. After further discussion, we concluded he could choose to improve his grades and concentrate on improving his math grade after all. He also decided he would practice relaxation and meditation at home with the intention of minimizing the tension between him and his grandmother.

During the following two weeks, Robert improved his performance in school, and his grandmother communicated to me that they were getting along much better. However, by the fourth week, he started declining in his schoolwork. He was losing motivation again, and he admitted that he felt like he needed to live with his mom or his dad.

After a meditation exercise to refocus his vision of graduating from high school and college, I told him we needed to explore additional ways to help himself meet his need for freedom and power. I had him think and write again about what would help him feel like he had more freedom and power. However, I told him I would like to try a different technique, one that would ensure he carried out the ideas he developed. In general, as one comes up with additional ideas, they require greater effort to carry them out. I did not want him to give up his desire without trying all possible options he had considered. He agreed. The technique I used is called the circle of commitment.

THE CIRCLE OF COMMITMENT

The circle of commitment is a technique in which, by your own decision, you agree to stay inside the circle until you make a choice that you are willing to carry out. No one will stop you from getting out of the circle at any time, even if you have not been able to make a choice.

You can perform this process on your own; however, it is helpful to have someone to share your thoughts and feelings with and ask you questions that can be helpful to you for making the commitment to carry out the choice(s) you are leaning toward. The person outside the circle cannot tell you what to do or not to do. He or she can only ask you questions that can help you make your own choice.

I asked Robert if he was willing to go through this process, and he agreed. I restated the purpose and the commitment he was making to himself and me about the circle and that he should only make a choice he would commit to carry out.

I directed him to sit on a chair, close his eyes, and imagine a circle on the floor around him. I asked him to take a few deep breaths until he felt relaxed. As he was relaxing, I stated again that the purpose of the circle was to come up with ideas that would help him feel like that he had more freedom and power, and to select the one(s) he was willing to commit to carrying out. He would remain in the circle until he selected at least one idea he would commit to carry out.

I asked him to open his eyes, handed him a sheet of paper, and asked him to take about fifteen minutes to think and write down actions he could chose to do to feel more freedom and power.

He came up with some ideas that included remaining in El Paso with his grandmother. After considering each choice, since his strongest desire was to live with one of his parents, he mentioned he had been thinking about speaking to his dad in San Antonio about allowing him to come live with him. He had asked before but had been told "no" by his father because he knew he had been misbehaving and he did not want nor had the time to deal with him being in trouble.

I asked Robert if there was any other choice he could make that could convince his father to let him live with him. He thought for a while and he responded, "I guess I could tell him that I am willing to continue meeting with a therapist or coach like you to help myself shape up. He may go for it." I asked him if he was willing to commit to 1) talking to his father and

2) following through with the coaching or counseling if his dad accepted the idea and he responded affirmatively.

I then asked him to close his eyes again, take a few deep breaths, and relax. I asked him to imagine himself speaking to his dad and mentioning his idea to him along with his willingness to continue coaching or counseling with a professional. He actually smiled as he was visualizing the possibility of going to live with his dad.

After that, I asked him to open his eyes. At this point I told him we needed to let his grandmother know of what he had chosen to do to get her feedback about his choice. He agreed. I reminded him again of his commitment. He acknowledged it, and I asked him to step out of the circle.

When his grandmother came to pick him up, we discussed it with her, and she agreed with his choice, hoping that his dad would accept. She stated that all she wanted was for him to be happy and graduate from high school and go to college.

YOUR SUCCESS JOURNEY

Now that we knew Robert would be moving to live with his father, I had him perform the "Your Success Journey" process. This process would help him further install in his mind the realization that for him to be able to remain with his father once he moved, he was to come through with his commitment to continue working with a therapist or coach. His dad wanted to be sure he would continue improving his behaviors to be able to graduate from high school with good grades to gain acceptance to college after high school.

The process works as follows:

1. Have a set of assorted-color crayons or colored pens, and a few sheets of 8.5 x 11" paper.

2. Write the desired final outcome on one sheet of paper with one or multiple colors you like. With some assistance from me, Robert wrote: *Attend and graduate from college.*

3. Write on separate sheets of paper the action steps you are responsible for taking in order to get to your final desired outcome. Use a different color of your liking to write down each action step. Robert wrote a) *Move in with my dad at the end of the semester,* b) *Look for a coach or therapist and start the process,* c) *Keep a good relationship with my dad and his girlfriend,* d) *Enroll in high school for the new school year,* e) *Apply myself in high school and graduate with a B+ or A grade average,* f) *Attend and graduate from college with honors.*

4. Place on the floor each sheet of paper you wrote in the order you will take each step, ending with the final outcome. Place each sheet of paper at a step's distance. Robert's steps looked like this:

Move in with my dad at the end of the semester	Look for a coach or therapist and start the process	Keep a good relationship with my dad and his girlfriend	Enroll in high school for the new school year	Apply myself in high school and graduate with a B+ or A average	Attend and graduate from college with honors

5. Now, stand over your final outcome sheet. Once you are standing over your final outcome, close your eyes and take a few deep breaths and feel relaxed. Place your dominant hand over your heart and repeat to yourself the following affirmation slowly three times: "I am totally responsible for achieving this outcome and I achieve it." Every time you repeat it, allow the meaning of this phrase to sink in your mind and in your heart.

6. Now, step off your final outcome and, starting with your first action step, repeat the same process with each step in your journey to achieving your final outcome. The affirmation changes to "I am totally responsible for executing this action step, and I do it." It

is important that you take your time, relax, and repeat the affirmation three times slowly as you walk and step over each action step. Remember to place your dominant hand on your heart at each step.

7. When you step over your final outcome, repeat the process as you did in Step 5.

This concludes your success journey, which is now part of your being — and because you have assumed total responsibility for it, you will achieve it. You can be certain of it. Total responsibility makes you unstoppable.

THE SELF-QUESTIONING PROCESS

One easy and effective method I use with my clients to help them make their own decisions and choices of action to resolve their issues is the self-questioning process. I use this approach from the outset and throughout each of my sessions. Sooner or later, the clients notice how the questioning pattern is repeated every time they express that they do not know what to do or feel confused about a problem or issue. They also notice how easy it is to arrive at making a choice that may yield the solution they are looking for.

The process has four steps and, just like I used it with Robert, you can use it by yourself whenever you need to come up with choices or solutions to improve any part of your life. This process is also called the WDEP model for getting what you want, and it was developed by Robert G. Hoglund. Robert is a prominent reality/choice therapist who also worked with Dr. Glasser and was one of my teachers during my reality/choice therapy certification journey.

Want: What is it that you want?

Doing: What are you doing?

Evaluate: Is it helping? Or Is it working?

Plan: What else can you do?

Very often when we are trying to find a solution to a problem or how to go about reaching a goal, we make choices that temporarily help us feel better but, sooner rather than later, we find out that was not what we really wanted, and the problem continues or arises again. When this happens, we go back to the model and ask again the four basic questions.

In the case of Robert, he initially wanted to improve his grades in school and the actions he chose to improve them worked for a while. The issue arose again after two weeks. Then he chose, along with his grandmother, to work on their relationship, and that also worked for a short period of time. Through our continued work and my questioning, he finally discovered what he really wanted was to move in with one of his parents.

This was the solution that satisfied his needs the most, and fortunately it worked for him. He was able to get what he wanted. However, what if his father had not accepted his proposal, or what if staying with his dad did not work in time? Robert now has a method by which he can continue to live his life knowing that he is responsible for it and that he can continue to make choices that yield new results. He has greater control of his life and in the process, he will learn that life is not perfect, and when facing imperfect results, he has the self-empowerment to continue making conscious choices. He knows his life is the way it is because of the results of the choices he has made, and he can always make new choices instead of giving his power up by letting others choose for him.

I desire the highest level of self-empowerment for you and every other human being. Realizing that blaming circumstances and others for the way your life is sabotages your own freedom, happiness, and peace.

Taking control of your life through your choices and activating those choices gives you the highest level of self-empowerment to live the life you are designed to live.

MY CHOICE TODAY

My choice today is to be happy.
To notice and enjoy the beauty God makes.
Even when life seems like an endless strife,
I'll keep an optimistic view of life.
This is my choice today.

My choice today is to smile.
To encourage those that I come in contact with.
To provide emotional support to others.
To keep a hopeful attitude and share it.
This is my choice today!

My choice today is to do the best job I can.
To be productive and be fair to my employer.
To do my duties diligently and do them
for the benefit of others. This is my choice today!

My choice today is not to make rushed decisions.
To first consider all possible alternatives.
To ask God for his guidance and discerning power,
and to take responsibility for the results of my choices.
This is my choice today!

My choice today is to be at peace with myself.
To realize that all I can do is my best.
To realize I can't control anything or anybody.
All I can do is my best and leave to God the rest.
This is my choice today!

My choice today is to be content.
Even in the midst of negative circumstances,
I'll be thankful for the good and bad.
The good, I'll enjoy and rejoice in it.
The bad, I'll use to gain strength and improve.
This is my choice today!

—Jose M. Baltazar, PhD

Yes, You Can Transform Your Life: Change Your Current Paradigm of Living to The Life Transformation Paradigm

"Aggressive action often produces exactly the opposite of what is intended. It produces instability and oscillation, instead of moving you more quickly toward your goal."

— Peter M. Senge, *The Fifth Discipline*

Everyone has a paradigm about living life. Most have as their paradigm the "work hard" paradigm. Another prevalent paradigm of living is the "live the life you want" paradigm.

These two popular paradigms — which, by the way, are preached by too many business and self-development "gurus" — have created the hurried and stressful lifestyle most people live today.

Some of the expressions you hear frequently from people who live under these paradigms are as follows:

- "You can't get ahead unless you work hard."
- "You have to be a go-getter."

- "You have to bust your butt at the beginning so you can enjoy the life you want later."
- "Money is not the most important thing in life, but it sure helps to have it."
- And so on.

The majority of people follow these paradigms, and they live their lives in a constant hurry and urgency following the "dream." They believe they must live a busy, hurried, and stressful life in order to prosper, and they end up feeling tired most of the time, dismayed, and sick from their stressful lifestyle.

Although these paradigms produce results, these results have been accomplished under so much stress that in the process the majority get sick from more than one chronic disease. As I stated in the foreword, the coronavirus pandemic will pass, but we forget that before this pandemic, we have had the stress pandemic for almost a century by now.

As a society, we have worked ourselves into so much stress that science now accepts that most chronic diseases have a strong connection to unhealthy levels of stress. And yet we are not alarmed that millions in the United States and perhaps billions in the world die from some type of chronic disease. One of the purposes of this book is to raise awareness about this fact. We should be alarmed, just as we are alarmed about the COVID-19 pandemic, and be motivated to prevent chronic disease, not through medications but through lifestyles that prevent the devastating damages stress produces in our lives.

For years I have been living by, and teaching and coaching others according to, my Life Transformation Paradigm. I have seen it work so many times that for the past five years or so, I thought of writing this book to share it with you and the world. My Life Transformation Paradigm is a holistic and systemic approach to living the busy and demanding life of today, but without the devastating damage stress causes in our lives. In addition, to help you live a productive life without harmful stress, another major difference of my model is that it works for all situations in life whether they have to do with finances, relationships, bad habits and addictions, mental/physical/spiritual problems, work and career, or any other situation you are trying to improve in your life.

I hope you take on the holistic health and wellness system my model promotes. Imagine realizing every desire in your life in a state of good health of mind/body/spirit. My model is a system of behavior that emphasizes stress reduction along with other productive ways of living life.

If you need guidance through the model and coaching through interventions designed for your specific circumstances, you can contact me at drjosembaltazar@gmail.com or www.josebaltazar.com. You can also find me on Facebook at Dr. Jose M Baltazar and join my group "Life Transformation: Living Healthy, Happy, Long, and Prosper Without Stress."

My best to you always.
— Dr. Jose M. Baltazar

REFERENCES

Asprey, Dave. *The Bulletproof Diet: Lose Up to a Pound a Day, Reclaim Energy and Focus, Upgrade Your Life*, 2014

Baltazar, Jose, Ph.D. *The Accelerated Learning Companion for College Students: Mind-Body Techniques to Make Your Learning Easier and Faster*, 2012

Barker, Joel. *The Power of Vision Training Manual*, 1990 https://starthrower.com/products/power-of-vision-joel-barker

Begley, Sharon. *Train Your MIND, Change Your BRAIN: How a New Science Reveals Our Extraordinary Potential to Transform Ourselves*, 2008

Benson, Herbert, M.D. *The Relaxation Response: A Simple Meditative Technique that Has Helped Millions Cope with Fatigue, Anxiety, and Stress*, 1976

Borynsenko, Joan, Ph.D. *Inner Peace for Busy People: 52 Simple Strategies for Transforming Your Life*, 2001

Batmanghelidj, Fereydoon, M.D. *Water for Health, for Healing, for Life: You're Not Sick, You're Thirsty*, 2003

Canfield, Jack, Mark Victor Hansen, and Less Hewitt. *The Power of Focus: How to Hit Your Business, Personal, and Financial Targets with Absolute Certainty*, 2000

Canfield, Jack, with Paul R. Shield. *Effortless Success: Living the Law of Attraction*. CD Audio Program, 2009

Catholic Book Publishing. *The New American Bible*, 2008

Coby, Stephen R. *The 7 Habits of Highly Effective People*, 1990

Dopart, Susan B. *A Recipe for Life: By the Doctor's Dietitian*, 2009

Dyer, Wayne. *Change Your Thoughts – Change Your Life: Living the Wisdom of the Tao*, 2007

Frankl, Victor E., M.D. *Man's Search for Meaning*, 1984

Fuhrman. Joel, M.D. *Eat to Live: The Amazing Nutrient-Rich Program for Fast and Sustained Weight Loss*, 2011

Glasser, William, M.D. *Choice Theory: A New Psychology of Personal Freedom*, 1998

Glasser, William, M.D. *Counseling with Choice: The New Reality Therapy*, 2001

Glasser, William, M.D. *Reality Therapy: A New Approach to Psychiatry*, 1975

Goleman, Daniel. *Emotional Intelligence: Why It Can Matter More Than I.Q.*, 1995

Hay, Louise. *You Can Heal Your Life*, 2004

Hay, Louise. *You Can Heal Your Life: Companion Book*, 2002

Hicks, Esther & Jerry. *The Law of Attraction: The Basics of the Teachings of Abraham*, 2006

Hicks, Esther & Jerry. *Ask and It is Given: Learning to Manifest Your Desires*, 2004

His Holiness Dalai Lama & Howard Cutler, M.D. *The Art of Happiness: A Handbook for Living*, 1998

Hogland, Robert G. *Questioning Process: The WDEP Model, Center for Quality Education Training Manual*, 2002

Howard, Pierce, J., Ph.D. *The Owner's Manual for the Brain: The Ultimate Guide for Peak Mental Performance at All Ages*, 2014

Kabat-Zinn, Jon. *Mindfulness for Beginners: Reclaiming the Present Moment and Your Life*, 2012

Kriyananda, Swami. *The Essence of the Bhagavad Gita*, 2006

Leyse-Wallace, Ruth, Ph.D. *Linking Nutrition to Mental Health: A Scientific Exploration*, 2008

Lipton, Bruce H., Ph.D. *The Biology of Belief: Unleashing the Power of Consciousness, Matter, and Miracles*, 2005

Morrissey, Brian M. *Brain State Mastery: Riding the Wave of Consciousness and the Brain to A Better Life*, 2006

Ostrander, Sheila, and Lynn Schroeder. *Super-Learning: Have a Supermemory! Improve Business and Sports Performance! Learn Anything Ten Times Faster*, 1982.

Ostrander, Sheila, and Lynn Schroeder. *Super-Learning 2000: New, Triple-Fast Ways You Can Learn, Earn, and Succeed in the 21st Century*, 1994.

Perlmutter, David, M.D. *Brain Grain: The Surprising Truth About Wheat, Carbs, and Sugar – Your Brain's Silent Killer*, 2013

Physical Exercise: Go to Pinterest.com or Youtube.com: Search for "Yoga Exercises," "Qi-Gong Exercises," "Tai-Chi Exercises," "Aerobic Workouts," "Brain Health workouts," or any other specific exercise interest. You have to include exercise in your Mind-Body-Spirit improvement plan.

Sapolsky, Robert M. *Why Zebras Don't Get Ulcers: The Acclaimed Guide to Stress, Stress-Related Disease, and Coping*, 2004

Schwartz, Mark S., & Frank Andrasik. *Biofeedback: A Practitioner's Guide*, 2003

Sears, Barry, Ph.D., with Bill Lawren. *Enter the Zone: A Dietary Road Map to Lose Weight Permanently, Reset Your Genetic Code, Prevent Disease, Achieve Maximum Physical Performance, Enhance Mental Productivity*, 1995

Seligman, Martin, E.P. *Authentic Happiness: Using the New Positive Psychology to Realize Your Potential for Lasting Fulfillment*, 2002

Seligman, Martin E.P. *Learned Optimism: How to Change Your Mind and Life*, 1991

Senge, Peter M. *The Fifth Discipline: The Art and Practice of the Learning Organization*, 1990

The Corporate Body of The Buddha Foundation. *The Seeker's Glossary of Buddhism*. 1998

TS Production, LLC. *The Secret (DVD): The Secret Has Traveled Through Centuries to Reach You*, 2006

Watt, Tessa. *Mindfulness: A Practical Guide*, 2012

Wubbolding, Robert E. *Reality Therapy for the 21st Century*, 2002

www.ingramcontent.com/pod-product-compliance
Lightning Source LLC
Chambersburg PA
CBHW071233210326
41597CB00016B/2038